The Complete
COCKATIEL

by
Dr. Matthew M. Vriends

First Edition — First Printing

1983

HOWELL BOOK HOUSE INC.
230 Park Avenue
New York, N.Y. 10169

Library of Congress Cataloging in Publication Data

Vriends, Matthew M., 1937–
  The complete cockatiel.

  Bibliography: p. 174
  1. Cockatiel. I. Title.
SF473.C6V74   1983   636.6'865   83-4351
ISBN 0-87605-817-9

Contents

As a pet, as an aviary bird and as the focal point of a fascinating hobby, the Cockatiel has become the popular favorite of countless bird enthusiasts. His winning combination of pleasing appearance and personable disposition have made him one of the world's favorite bird pets.

Photo by Kelley, from ALL ABOUT THE PARROTS, © 1980 by Arthur Freud and reproduced with the permission of the publisher, Howell Book House Inc.

Preface

IT IS A WELL-KNOWN FACT that Cockatiels (*Nymphicus hollandicus*) make excellent aviary and cage birds, and even a beginner should have little difficulty in keeping a pair (or even more). Not only are they endowed with beautiful coloring, but with a noble crest and a fine build as well, making them great favorites among aviculturists.

A friend of mine puts it very well when he says:

"The Cockatiel is simply a gorgeous bird; nothing more, nothing less. The bird spends the largest part of his day on the perches, with an occasional playful flight from one perch to another. It is amusing to watch him amble across his perches, voicing his characteristic muttering. It sounds as if he is mumbling to himself. Tolerance is, no doubt, his best virtue, both towards his keeper and to all kinds of birds, both large and small. He is really very good-natured, and would never harm any of the other inhabitants."

Cockatiels are also noted for characteristically high intelligence. My Cockatiels whistle throughout the day, and the male, in particular, is capable of perfectly imitating a wide variety of other bird sounds. For a long time I thought that my Pekin Nightingale was whistling his tune, until I noticed that it was my Cockatiel that was singing so beautifully.

When I feed my Cockatiel, he will bravely remain on his perch, even when I am just a few inches away from him. Finally, I am so close that his bill is near my forehead. If, at this close range, I then whistle to him—like exchanging so much gossip—he always answers by whistling the same tune back to me.

The Cockatiel is the only representative of his genus. Because of his crest, the small cere on the bill, and the cheek markings, one could place him in the Cockatoo group, although his slender shape points to a close relationship with the Rosella species. In fact, as we will see in this book, the Cockatiel belongs somewhere between these two groups, though recently the tendency has been to classify this beautiful bird closer to the Cockatoos. Formerly it was classified under the genus *Leptolophus* (*leptos* = delicate, *lophos* = crest or plume).

In Australia the Cockatiel is very common in the wild, and I have, for instance, seen him many times around Adelaide. The birds' graceful, somewhat curved flight is fast, and when seen as dark silhouettes against the sky, they somewhat resemble Sparrow Hawks. Their excellent flight capacities are due to their narrow, slender wings and the long tail with three, four or five extremely long central feathers. They also stand out because of their decorative crest.

I have seen wild Cockatiels perched on telegraph wires and other electric cables in small villages and towns. They like to spend time in the so-called parklands, although they fly away as soon as they are approached, but will then circle around and return to their resting place. Practically every Sunday morning, when my wife and I were on our way to church, taking a short cut through these parklands, we would come across a certain pair perched on the telegraph wires (which are still, just as in the United States, strung across wooden poles). As soon as we would stop the car they would fly up, circle around, but very quickly return to their own little spot, glaring at us with crests raised! They live a nomadic existence, migrating to whatever regions offer the most food. Sometimes they can be seen in groups of several hundreds; a few decades ago they could even be observed in flocks of several thousands, according to Cayley.

This book contains, in compact and eminently readable form, practically everything anyone, long-experienced aviculturists or beginning fanciers alike, could wish to know on this subject. There are chapters on nomenclature, housing, feeding, and of course on the Cockatiel himself; how to breed him and what colors to expect. This book will enable owners, regardless of their degree of experience, to give their birds the care they deserve.

As stated before, Cockatiels are among the most popular aviary birds we have today. They are particularly well suited for anyone just beginning to keep birds, for they demand little in the way of care and are easy to breed. But Cockatiels can also win the hearts of experienced bird breeders because they offer endless opportunities to achieve fascinating color varieties through breeding experimentation. The Cockatiel is indeed a bird that gives *everybody* pleasure.

The object of this book is to discuss in simple terms the many phases of the interesting hobby of keeping and breeding Cockatiels; the information presented has been gained through many years of experience in breeding all types of parrots and parakeets, and also from much research work, as I am a biologist/ornithologist by profession. I have called on every possible resource available in order to make this book not only authoritative, but also interesting enough to warrant its being read and enjoyed by both beginning and experienced aviculturists.

MATTHEW M. VRIENDS

ACKNOWLEDGMENTS

I AM INDEBTED to the many aviculturists and curators of zoological societies who replied so helpfully to my requests for information and pictures, especially my friends Mr. and Mrs. Remi Ceuleers-Leysen, Herentals (A.), Belgium; Mr. D. Wissink, Doetinchem, Holland; Mr. Paul Kwast, editor of *Vogelvreugd,* Holland, and especially my friend Mr. P. E. Roders, D.V.M., Chairman of the Dutch Parrot Society. My grateful thanks are due to Mr. Seymour Weiss, Editor of Howell Book House Inc., New York, for his skilled editing, and to my dear friend Mrs. Ruth Hanessian, of Animal Exchange (Rockville, Maryland), for her ready help in all matters relating to this book.

I should also like to thank my wife, Mrs. Lucy Vriends-Parent for her invaluable assistance and patience during the preparation of the text; without her this book could never have been written.

All the opinions and conclusions expressed in the following pages are my own, however, and any errors are my own responsibility.

M.M.V.

A pair of Cockatiels in the wild.   *Roders*

1

The Avian Kingdom

The nurse in the office of a doctor who has one of my cockies wrote to tell me that a young American soldier came to see the doctor and was surprised and delighted to see a cockatiel strutting around the office. He said that he had been stationed on an island off Australia and in many places the birds were as thick as the English sparrow is in the United States. In fact, he said that many of the boys in his camp had made pets of this very friendly and intelligent bird and could be seen parading through the village, each one with a pet cockie riding on his shoulder. They did not try to keep them in captivity, and often all a soldier had to do was to whistle and his "own" pet would come flying out of the forest to him.

Mrs. E. L. Moon in
Experiences with my Cockatiels
(Copyright © 1976, TFH Publications)

AVICULTURE IS A HOBBY which gives many people great pleasure. It provides an opportunity not only to observe and study birds at close range, but also to enjoy their lively songs and brilliant colors. Birds made to feel comfortable and at ease will show themselves at their finest. Therefore, it is important to know about the particular characteristics, habits and general requirements of each species housed. In successful aviculture, captive conditions must represent, as closely as possible, those to which birds are accustomed in the wild.

11

History and Evolution

Before considering the particular care required by Cockatiels kept in captivity, it is worth having a quick look at the way in which all birds may have evolved from a reptilian ancestor nearly 200 million years ago. The word "evolution" means "gradual change" and although humans have understood for many centuries that it takes place, it is only recently —during this century—that they have come to understand the genetic mechanisms involved.

The theory of evolution by natural selection was first expounded by Charles Darwin (1809-1882) in 1859 when his famous book, *The Origin of Species* was published. In it he showed that the gradual change of simple forms of life into more complex ones might have been brought about by a succession of small steps covering millions of years.

This theory, which is now universally accepted, provides an explanation for the adaptation of plants and animals to their environments, and it further implies that if an organism is not well adapted it will soon become extinct. But environments usually change slowly (continental drift is a good example of this) and organisms adapt over successive generations of genetic mutation.

As a result of this lengthy process, the last few hundred million years have seen a multitude of plants and animal species gradually evolving.

The process by which species evolve is highly complex and difficult to understand without a thorough appreciation of the genetic mechanisms of inheritance. But a simplified explanation is possible, especially if we consider only those animals which reproduce sexually (as opposed to asexually when only one adult produces offspring). Birds reproduce sexually and for this purpose male and female adults combine their genetic material in the form of a hard-shelled egg which is incubated outside the body (they are therefore said to be oviparous). The developing chick is made up of characteristics of both parents and, although it will grow to be very like them, it will carry what are called individual differences. This because things can go wrong in the process by which one chick is made up from the characteristics of two adults. The "wrong" bit is called a mutation and yet sometimes it can actually be beneficial to the offspring that carries it. This chick might find that its mutation enabled it to see better than others around it. It would, therefore, be able to spot food or predators first and this factor would increase its survival chances. Increased survival opportunities gives it a better chance of breeding and, because the advantageous mutation has become a fixed part of its genetic make up, its own offspring will inherit genes for better vision. And so it goes on, generation after generation with mutations occurring in all parts of the body until some groups of individuals have changed in a way that not only makes them unrecognizable as closely related to the species to which they once

12

belonged, but also unable to breed with any living individuals from that species. They have, in effect, formed a new species.

Today, some 8600 bird species exist. There were once many more, perhaps a third as many again, but they have declined in the last few million years. All the countless subspecies of birds are simply changes being presently undertaken within species groups. In other words, a subspecies is a recognizable trend within a species towards the formation of a new species. Hybrid zones are made up when changing individuals breed with the individuals belonging to the original stock.

Another example can be drawn from reptiles. Lizards once lived primarily on the ground with many other different kinds of animals. Some lizards would have started to venture up the rough bark of trees. Many couldn't have stayed in the trees long because they were better suited to running over the earth below. But mutations for long sharp claws would have given tree-climbing advantages to some species. In the trees they would have found insects and safety from ground-dwelling predators; in other words, their chances of survival and reproduction were increased. Their offspring carried the same mutation and obviously lived in the tree-climbing manner of their parents. But now that they were in the trees other mutations were occurring and being selected for. They grew to look very different from their ground-dwelling ancestors. In time, new species were formed.

It is quite a good idea to examine reptile evolution, because it was from this group of animals that birds evolved some 160 million years ago. It is a complicated process and one about which we do not know a great deal. However, we can get some idea of the events that took place by tracing the outline of development.

Two-hundred and twenty million years ago the dry land was inhabited by insects, amphibians and reptiles. The latter group included the *Thecodonts* which were lizard-like creatures with very long tails. One group of Thecodonts adapted to life in the trees, with their forelegs becoming useful for climbing. In general their limbs enabled them to jump from branch to branch until they were quite at home many feet above the ground.

At some stage their reptilian scales began to assume a feathery appearance. This may have been to increase their insulation against cooling temperatures, but, whatever the reason, the tree-dwelling reptile became lighter and more able to undertake spectacular leaps from branch to branch and even from tree to tree. As they jumped they beat their feathery forelegs and this increased the distance they could travel through the air. The advantages of being able to do this were evidently selected for (perhaps they could out-distance predators or out-distance competitors for food) and their appearance became genetically "fixed". It was from this kind of beginning that birds evolved from reptiles.

The earliest known bird is *Archaeopteryx lithographica,* which means

13

"ancient winged creature, drawn into stone." The remarkable likeness between this bird and early flying reptiles (Saurians) can be seen in four limestone fossils found in Bavaria (Germany). Its anatomy was very much like a Saurian, but externally it looked much more like a bird because it possessed feathers. Close examination of its skeleton reveals a remarkable likeness between its feet and those of the little *Ornitholestes* dinosaur. The fact that the hind feet of both animals were talon-like suggests a similar lifestyle. They climbed onto branches of trees and bushes and from there, like parachutists, started their simple gliding flights.

The very first flights took place from above to below. The long midbone in the foot also suggests that the bird was capable of big, strong jumps. We can assume that the primitive bird lived in mountainous areas among bushes and rocks. The most important ingredient of this habitat was, of course, water in the form of inland lakes where many·types of animals lived. The fact that it had pointed teeth suggests that the primitive bird was a bird of prey, although it probably lived on the abundant supply of insects available. Birds became toothless rather late in the history of life on earth.

Little is known about the color of their feathers. It is popularly assumed that they were white or red-brown. Similarly, there is no evidence of the sort of nests built by the birds or the appearance of their eggs. Because *Archaeopteryx* is more bird-like than reptile-like, it is assumed that the eggs had hard shells.

There are a multitude of unanswered questions regarding the evolution of birds. Unfortunately their fragile bones are poorly preserved as fossils. When a bird died, its remains were usually scattered by other creatures living off carrion. To increase their powers of flight by weight reduction avian bones are light and hollow and so disintegrate fairly quickly. The petrification process or the formation of imprints in stone takes centuries. A bird skeleton seldom had enough time to turn into stone before it decomposed completely. From the Cretaceous period to the present time—an enormous period of time of approximately 65 million years—there are no fossil remains of land birds which might enable the reconstruction of these creatures. Only a few examples of water birds from this period have been found including a very lean duck-like bird and *Ichthyornis victor,* a little wading bird. The duck-like creature is one of the few aquatic birds from the Cretaceous period of which reconstructions could be made. It must have been an excellent flier with strong, well-developed wings. Its flying muscles were extremely well-developed, as was the large ridge on its breastbone to which the flight muscles were attached. It had to move its wings constantly in flight, that is, it could fly only actively. But this also meant that its flight ability was continuously developing. *Ichthyornis victor* had nearly the same characteristics. Its head was rather big, its beak enormous and it had little sharp conical teeth. Whether it had smaller or bigger swimming membranes than the present-day duck is not known. It represented the typical intermediate form of the aquatic bird. The tarsal bone of its feet was shorter than the shin bone (tibiatarsus) with its foot skeleton's position and development having more likeness to a wading foot rather than a swimming foot. It is often assumed that pre-historic animals looked like monsters, but *Ichthyornis victor* had nothing monster-like about it. It was no more than 8-10 in. (20-25 cm) high and its body length measured about 6 in. (14 cm). One could have kept it in a birdhouse! But it was a different matter with *Hesperornis regalis,* an ancestral diving bird which was 6 ft. (2 m) long. The wingstumps of *Hesperornis regalis* are relatively smaller than the ones of birds living today. It had sharp conical teeth with which it must have hunted fishes and cuttle-fish. The big sea-divers of today are assumed to be direct descendants of *Hesperornis regalis.*

From this general look at the origin of a few bird types we can see how some living birds might have arrived at their present-day form and function. But, as mentioned earlier, the fossil record for most birds is very poor and when we look around the world at all the differently-adapted kinds, we can do no more than wonder at the stages through which their ancestors might have passed. Evolution is a slow process and, of course, in the birds that we know, it is still happening today. If changes are occurring in the birds that we know, it is impossible for us to detect them. All we can do is observe and wonder at their adaptions which seem so "fixed", as though they have been in existence for millions of years. Among some examples of bird specialists are swifts which are renowned fliers and have completely developed wings, but useless feet. Ducks and geese, which are also good fliers, possess strong breast muscles and firm leg-combs. Swans, excellent swimmers and fliers, can move only with difficulty on land on their relatively weak feet. Chickens have strong legs and are slowly losing their flying ability. Pheasants, quails and other poultry will suffer the same fate. Many wading birds move around on long legs enabling them to wade far into the water in search of food without getting their plumage wet. Other clear forms of adaptation to environment and food are to be seen in beak forms, feathers, nest construction, development of chicks and the fact that there are birds of passage, resident birds and migratory birds. Life is far too short to see the changes in the evolution process, but those who are aware that this is going on, will no doubt continue to discover exciting aspects of ornithology and aviculture.

The development of birds to the forms which we now know took place during the Tertiary period which lasted from 60 million years ago until one million years ago. The climax of this progress took place during the Pliocene phase at the end of the Tertiary period.

15

The Living Bird

A bird's plumage is its most distinctive feature which, as already mentioned, was derived in the course of evolution from the scales of reptiles. Feathers are extremely fine creations of horn which protect the body. There are several kinds of feathers, each modified to serve a special use. Downy feathers conserve body heat and the top feathers smooth the bird's body contours into a streamlined shape. These contour feathers are distributed in well-defined feathertracts. In some species, like the woodpecker, tail feathers developed into means of support. The color of feathers is determined by either the pigment in the feather or the microscopic structure of the feather. Common pigments are the melanins, ranging from yellow-brown to black, and the lipochromes, ranging from yellow to red. Blue and other brilliant colors are the result of certain feather structures. The fact that rib cage and lumbar vertebrae are one unit is of great importance because the very important flight muscles are attached to it, as is the high breastbone comb. In the wings we clearly recognize the forelimbs of their ancestors, the reptiles. In many birds, the breast muscles may be as much as 15-20 percent of their total weight. The many neck vertebrae make the neck long and flexible, since the head and beak had to take over the function of the earlier front legs as the wings were developing. The bill manipulates food and nest material, feeds the young and is a weapon against attackers. The high body temperature (about 104° F [41° C]) is maintained by an efficient heart and circulatory system which, like the respiratory system, shows special adaptation. The rather small lungs connect with various air-sacs which make a bird's system of breathing a very effective one. Furthermore these air-sacs take care of warmth, insulation and weight reduction. As a result of high energy consumption, the bird's need for nourishment is great. Most birds have extremely good eyesight, with a visual acuity of six to eight times that of man. Most are dependent upon their eyes for finding their food, for detecting predators and for recognizing their mates. An exception to this rule, from New Zealand, is the nocturnal Kiwi which has reduced and rather short-sighted eyes. As a compensation it has well-developed hearing and scenting ability.

Distribution

Because of their ability to adapt, birds spread all over the world. With continuous adjustments new species were created and old ones became extinct. This development still takes place today. Again and again birds adapt to new circumstances and if they do not succeed they are condemned to extinction.

The greatest numbers and species of birds are found in tropical and sub-tropical areas.

The habitat of most species is limited to certain geographical areas: tanagers and hummingbirds are found only in North and South America (neotropical fauna); mousebirds are found only in Africa, south of the Sahara (ethiopic fauna); by far the greatest number of pheasant and babbler species occurs in southeast Asia (oriental fauna); emu and birds of paradise are typical representatives of the Australasian fauna. Closer to home, the dunnock has its habitat in the palearctic fauna, i.e. Europe, Asia up to the Himalayas and North Africa. This demonstrates that it is rare for one species to spread over a large part of the world. The exceptions are a few species of water-based birds and some birds of prey.

Sparrows and starlings can today be found in Australia and in the northern United States because they were imported from Europe in the 19th Century. All birds are adapted to their environments and they cannot live successfully in those which are different, a fact which a bird-keeper must never lose sight of. Thus, there are limits to their range of distribution. Keeping and breeding birds, including Cockatiels, successfully can be achieved only if they are given good care and compatible environments (i.e. suitable birdhouses) where their natural habitats are re-created as successfully as possible with the right food and appropriate cage companions. If we do not comply with these requirements, birds in birdhouses will suffer the same problems as their counterparts in the wild. As a result of many landscape changes believed by man to be necessary, bird numbers have declined. Birds have become so-called culture-escapists. By luck, it also sometimes happens that birds adapt to new situations and thus become culture-followers, as for example Cockatiels! But the question must be asked whether such changes will, sooner or later, have a detrimental effect on the number of currently viable species.

The Development of Aviculture

It is not known where birds were first kept in captivity, but it must have been long before man could express himself in wall paintings or writing on parchment. There is evidence in the cultural history of both the old and new world to indicate that birds were kept by many different races. Paintings and hieroglyphics left behind by ancient Egyptians contain many references to doves, parrots, ducks and ibises as well as other birds used for hunting ducks, snipes and herons.

Silk paintings, vases and other ceramic objects of the ancient Chinese portray a rich collection of colorful birds. If the illustrations are to be interpreted correctly, most of the birds shown were domesticated. It is assumed that the history of the domestic chicken goes back at least 5000 years to the first township in India. The chicken, descended from the Red Jungle Fowl (*Gallus gallus*) which still lives in the bamboo forests of southeast Asia, was carried by man to all parts of the world. Today more than

17

200 different breeds are known, from the Bantam to the most beautiful Onagodori, a Japanese breed with a fantastic tail, often as much as six feet in length.

The Incas in South America also took an interest in birds and even tamed some species, such as the Amazon Parrots, which they kept in their houses and temples. Therefore, we can assume that birds are among the oldest domesticated animals. Over the centuries, the practice of keeping and caring for birds grew. But the reasons for keeping them changed continually. For instance, hawks and falcons were used to capture other birds and small mammals. Falconry is a sport that has been known for many centuries.

When nomadic people gradually settled, they had more time at their disposal for wall paintings and carving which often depicted courageous deeds carried out during hunting. Drawings of various birds still exist from this period. When man discovered that some birds also provide food, Falcons and other hunting birds became less popular, and instead the breeding of chickens began. Today the chicken provides one of the cheapest forms of meat. In the United States each year, more than two billion chickens are produced. The number of laying hens in America alone is more than twice the world's human population: more than 640 million eggs are sold yearly. Selective breeding has also increased egg-yield. A hen at the time of Roman civilization laid 50 to 60 eggs a year, whereas today the world record for eggs laid by one hen in a year is 361.

In the Near East, the pigeon must have established itself as a common garden or park bird in ancient times. Today the total number of pigeons cannot even be estimated. The pigeon has been used for various purposes for thousands of years: messenger services, food and decoration, and pigeon-racing has become a world-wide sport.

However, pigeons have also become a major nuisance in most of the world's larger cities. Their excreta is a constant threat to public health and it also does great damage to buildings. But it is not only the pigeon that has become distributed in such great numbers over the whole world. The millions of Canaries, Budgerigars, Cockatiels and Zebra finches kept in cages and aviaries are more numerous than the entire stock of wild Canaries, Budgerigars, Cockatiels and Zebra finches in the Canary Islands and Australia, from where European seamen first brought these birds in the 15th and 19th centuries.

The close relationship between man and birds has existed throughout history. There are a number of incidents recorded in the Bible which illustrate the roles of birds as friends or companions to man. The dove has always been a symbol of peace. In ancient Egypt, much care was lavished on various water birds, which were kept in specially constructed ponds, particularly in the nobility's large gardens or close to their temples. A statue of the Egyptian diety Horus of Shahom, in the shape of a falcon, stands as a massive monument among the columns of Edfu. The Egyptians also built huge bird-cages in the large houses of the rich which were filled with numerous songbirds and parrots. Pigeons were already kept at that time. In earlier times, the nobility and members of the higher Indian castes possessed aviaries where they bred not only songbirds, but also different kinds of parrots and parakeets. Some birds were even regarded as having priceless value and a man was appointed exclusively to look after them. We also know that the old Egyptians brought parakeets from India with the intention of breeding them in specially constructed birdhouses. Some years later, Alexander the Great brought the first Rose-ringed Parakeets to Europe after seeing them on his travels through India. In the Middle Ages, monks kept caged birds not only to study their behavior, but also to sell them to royalty. From there on the hobby of aviculture gradually developed in Europe. In the 15th and 16th centuries, both rich and poor started to keep many species of native songbirds.

The best known songbird is probably the Canary which the Spaniards were already breeding in the 15th century. The Budgerigar is a relatively new cage bird, introduced to England in 1840 by the bird artist, John Gould, and a few years later on the Continent; the same applies for the Cockatiel! Much has happened to these two small parrots since then.

During the days when European seamen crossed the seas in huge sailing vessels, they would often bring birds back with them as presents for their wives and children. Among the most popular were parrots and parakeets from South America, where they had been domesticated some centuries earlier.

In the ancient empires of China and Japan, quite a number of hard and softbills were kept in the cages and aviaries of palaces. Rich collections of water birds are shown on many silk paintings as well as being delicately carved in wood and ivory. These are the countries of origin for many birds now kept by aviculturists. An example is *Lonchura domestica*. During its period of domestication (which can be traced back to about 1700), different varieties were bred and it finally became a very popular ornamental bird. It came to Europe quite late: to England in 1860, to Germany in 1872 and to Holland in 1874. We don't know when it came to America. On its arrival, it quickly gained wide acceptance among bird breeders.

One of the last species to become completely domesticated was the Cockatiel of Australia. We propose to look in detail at this beautiful bird.

Aviculturists often find themselves having to justify the practice of keeping birds in captivity, especially to members of animal protection societies. Critics maintain that caged birds are deprived of their freedom and are dependent on the goodwill of their owners, and that the birds' welfare is therefore subject to human whims and degrees of efficiency and benevolence.

19

It is undeniable that in the past birds which would have been better off left in the wild were kept in captivity, and that cruel practices occurred for the amusement of bird owners. Present-day bird enthusiasts should therefore try to understand the arguments of people who are opposed to the caging of birds. Both are motivated by the same feelings, a love of Nature in general and birds in particular.

Today aviculturists play an important role in the conservation of bird species. With increasing pollution, de-forestation, and the drainage of swamps, ponds, rivers and lakes, the environment is being slowly destroyed, with little consideration for the many forms of life which are thus threatened with extinction. It is thanks to zoos that many species have been saved from dying out, and thanks to the aviculturists that many birds have been preserved for future generations.

Sympathy for caged animals is entirely misplaced. The great number of nests full of chicks which appear every year in aviaries show that aviary birds cannot be suffering unduly from being in captivity. They have many enemies and predators in the wild, human beings included, and their natural habitats are slowly being encroached upon by civilization. Naturalists have studied how birds which at one time were found only in the forests have moved to parks and later into towns. Some species totally vanish from sight if they are not able to move on when their habitat is encroached upon.

For many centuries, man has kept domesticated animals, including birds; not only to provide food but also for the aesthetic pleasure they provide.

Included among the birds which have long been domesticated are geese, ducks, chickens, guinea fowl, turkeys and pigeons. Canaries, Budgerigars, Cockatiels, Bengalese and Zebra-finches have been kept in captivity slightly less long. Other species in the process of becoming domesticated are lovebirds (*Agapornidae*), Turquoisine parakeets, Bourke's parakeets, Quaker (Monk or Gray-breasted) parakeets, African ringneck and many Grass-finches (from Australia), among others.

To believe that birds suffer untold anguish when confined in a cage or aviary is to "humanize" them; human beings suffer in captivity because behind bars or barbed wire they imagine how beautiful freedom would be; but such imagination is only possessed by humans. Animals live mainly for the present, are happy and satisfied if they have enough to eat and drink, sufficient light, plenty of room to move and exercise, opportunity to reproduce and protection from their enemies and bad weather. An escaped bird will often return to its cage or aviary of its own accord. Many people think that a bird would fly away jubilantly if its cage or aviary door were opened, but in fact the bird would probably feel rather bewildered, unsure and inhibited.

20

Provided that birds are properly cared for, there should be no criticism of keeping them in cages and aviaries. The majority of owners lavish care and attention on their birds, go out of their way to provide them with the most appropriate food; and so create a little piece of Nature where birds can build their nests without restraint or disturbance, and rear their young with a ready supply of food.

Cockatiels roam together in large flocks over the grass and lightly timbered country of inland Australia. They like to nest in the hollow limbs of trees near or even in water. The female lays four to seven, usually five, white eggs. Both sexes incubate the eggs; the male from early morning until late afternoon. *Photo by author*

22

2

The Cockatiel
Becomes Civilized

AUSTRALIAN PARROTS AND PARAKEETS have been enjoying the limelight for over 300 years. Seafarers, explorers, ornithologists and biologists alike, as well as aviculturists, have been enchanted by these birds. During the seventeenth century, sailors and travellers of the Dutch East India Company noted many different bird species while sailing along what is now known as the coast of Western Australia; I would rather not speak of the less fortunate among them whose ships were wrecked on the rocks and who were washed ashore on the little coastal islands. . . .

In 1697 Vlamingh landed near the mouth of the Swan River, which he named after finding many Black Swans there, several of which he managed to capture, and two of which he brought back alive to Batavia! As early as 1688 Dampier had come across various different and interesting birds near Cygnet Bay in the northwest regions of Australia. It is little wonder that in 1699, in his famous discovery ship *Roebuck,* he observed large quantities of birds near the estuary of the Swan River, as well as at what was later called the Dampier Archipelago in Western Australia.

As far as can be ascertained, it was in 1770 that the first observations were made of bird life in eastern Australia by the natural sciences research-ing team of Bank and Solander, who visited "down under" (Australia) together with Cook in the *Endeavour.* It is most likely that Cook and his people were the first Europeans to observe the Cockatiel in what is currently

New South Wales. Cook brought various bird species back to England; he made his selections from several locations, ranging from Botany Bay near Sydney to the Endeavour River in northern Queensland. The specimens brought back to England, as well as the large collection of fairly accurate drawings (many in color), generated a great deal of interest. This interest was not just confined to England, and the enthusiasm grew steadily with the first settlers near Sydney in 1788. This time period is also earmarked by the intensive research for life opportunities and colonization that took place.

No doubt John Gould and his very talented wife, Elisabeth, can be credited for inspiring enthusiasm for Australian fauna among a great many people in their time. It was Elisabeth, in fact, who was responsible for the greatest number and the most beautiful of their illustrations. Their visit to Australia between 1838 and 1840 resulted in the splendid, well known Gould bird books, among them *The Birds of Australia*. Apparently, during Gould's time there was no shortage of Cockatiels, because in his typical, somewhat ponderous prose, he says:

> I have seen the ground quite covered with them while engaged in procuring food, and it was no unusual circumstance to see hundreds together on the dead branches of gum trees in the neighbourhood of water, a plentiful supply of which appear to be essential to their existence.

A hand-painted picture of the Cockatiel made in 1840, when the Goulds were still in Australia, can be found in Volume X of *The Naturalist Library*. In this volume the Cockatiel is referred to as the Red Cheeked Nymphious, scientifically known as *Nymphious Novae Hollandiae*, Wagler. And although the naming seems a little strange, the color picture eliminates any doubt . . . it is the Cockatiel they are describing. Yet further perusal of this volume reveals a decidedly limited knowledge of the Cockatiel at that time, because it states:

> . . . . it does not appear to be a numerous species, as few specimens have yet found their way into our museums, and no detailed accounts of its natural history have hitherto been recorded. It is a native of New Holland of what particular district we are ignorant. It is likely that this bird and its congeners will constitute the rasorial type of this sub-family. In the lengthened tail feathers of this genus an analogy or distant affinity to the Ring Parrakeets, with which the illustrations were concerned, may be traced.

In this connection it is interesting to mention Cassel's *Book of Birds*, Part I (actually a translation of the German bird book by Dr. Brehm), dating from the end of the nineteenth century, which shows a number of outstanding illustrations of a pair of Cockatiels by a drinking place in their natural habitat. Following *The Naturalist Library's* lead, this book also refers to the Cockatiel scientifically as *Nymphious Novae Hollandiae*, as well as the name Corella, which was already then widely used. After giving a detailed description of both the male and female, Dr. Brehm continues with:

> Gould, whom we have to thank for a full description of the Corella, found this beautiful bird in great numbers in the interior of Australia. On the coast it is rare in comparison with the thousands seen on the plains of the interior, and in eastern Australia it seems to be more numerous than in the western parts of that Continent. In summer the Corellas make their nests near the Hunter and Peel rivers, and other streams running north, if they can find suitable trees. After the breeding season they assemble in innumerable flocks, which cover whole tracts of country, or alight in hundreds upon the overhanging branches of the gum trees . . . They devour grass seed, but cannot live without water, and, thereby, must remain in the neighbourhood of a stream . . .

Domestication

Until this time, of course, no books had yet appeared on the market describing the Cockatiel as a cage and aviary bird. In the beginning of the twenties, however, the magazine *Cage Birds* published a book entitled *Budgerigars and Cockatiels,* written by C. P. Arthur, who refers to the Cockatiel as *Calopsittacus novae-hollandiae.* Apart from "Cockatiel" other names mentioned, such as "Crested Ground Parrakeet", "Grey Parrot" and "Yellow top-knotted Parrot." It is noteworthy that the name "Cockatoo Parrot" was not yet being used, and we will delve into this more deeply later on. Naturally, a great deal of the information in C. P. Arthur's book was extracted from the book written by Gould; further he states: ". . . . with the exception of the north-east corner of Queensland, they range practically over the whole of Australia. Quarrion and Top-knot Parrakeet are their Australian names. . ."

Both the scientific naming—more on this in the next paragraph— as well as the English naming apparently caused quite some consternation. For quite a while there was disagreement over the spelling, some using "Cockatiel," while others preferred "Cockateel." In a later book, also published by *Cage Birds,* Westley T. Page uses the scientific name *Calopsittacus novae-hollandiae* and the English name "Cockateel." In the thirties *The Parrot Book,"* by Allen Silver, was published by Marshall Press Ltd. Silver speaks of the "Cockatiel" and uses the scientific name *Leptolophus hollandious,* a name which appears in the 1948 publication of Serventy and Whittel *Birds of Western Australia*; they also speak of "Cockatoo Parrot" and "Weero," the last name being one of the many used by the Aborigines. According to Ian Harman (in: *Australian Parrots in Bush and Aviary,* Inkata Press, Melbourne and Sydney, 1981), the scientific name *Psittacus hollandicus* was also used, and specifically by Kerr in his *Animal Kingdom* (1792), while Newton's *Dictionary of Birds* (1896) tells us that the name "Cockatiel" was first used by a bird merchant in London, but that he (Newton) prefers the spelling "Cockateel." He continues with:

> . . . .A bird-fancier's name lately invented by Mr. Jamrach and now in common use, being an English adaptation of "Kakatieltje," which in its turn is supposed to be a Dutch sailor's rendering of the Portuguese word "Cacatitho" or "Cacatelho," meaning a little Cockatoo.

The well known *Parrots in Captivity* by Dr. W. T. Greene, which was published in three parts between 1884 and 1887 (a fourth part was printed in an extremely limited edition for reasons I am not aware of, and only a few museums have a copy), uses the name "Cockatiel" and *Psittacus Novae-Hollandiae,* Russ, and as anyonyms *Palaeornis Novae-Hollandiae, Leptolopus auricomis, Nymphacus Novae-Hollandiae* and *Calopsitta Novae-Hollandiae,* Gould. During the fifties, the well known aviculturist, Mr. Alec Brooksbank, of the famous Keston Foreign Bird Farm, published his *Foreign Birds for Garden Aviaries,* using the scientific nomenclature also used by Allen Silver. In 1956, Brooksbank's partner, Mr. E. J. Boosey, suddenly started using "Cockatiel" and *Nymphicus hollandicus* in all his articles and books, and these are the names that we use today.

You may now no longer see the forest for the trees, and really are not all that interested in this nomenclature confusion. Yet we can draw certain conclusions from all the above, one being that it is very clear that around 1884 the Cockatiel was well known as a breeding bird in England as well as on the Continent under the name of "Cockatiel." In 1902 David Seth-Smith writes in the book *Parrakeets* that the Cockatiel is so very well known that a description is hardly necessary ("So well is this Parrakeet known, even to the veriest tyro in aviculture, that a description seems almost unnecessary. . ."). A survey held by Seth-Smith at the beginning of the century revealed that after Budgerigars, Cockatiels were the birds most likely to be found in English aviaries! He even stated that it was possible to have four or more broods per season (during spring and summer) and mentioned a specific example of a pair that raised sixteen young between March and September, which for that time in particular, was a great success:

> It [the Cockatiel] will breed readily in any aviary, and even in a cage sometimes, laying four or five eggs, which are frequently all hatched. Often four or more broods are produced during the spring and summer, so that it can well be imagined that a pair of Cockatiels will soon add very considerably to the population of an aviary. A pair kept by the writer a few years ago reared sixteen young birds between March and September, brood after brood being produced in the same nest-box, the female often commencing to lay again before the young left the nest, in which case it was necessary, as soon as the young had flown, to carefully remove and wash the eggs, replacing them after cleaning out the nest-box.

Typical Cockatiel pair showing the male (cock) at left with the female (hen) at right. The basic color of these small natives of Australia is gray with white markings across the wings. *Drawing by the author*

Cockatiels do not seem to mind their nest being examined, or, if necessary, cleaned out; true, they make a good deal of noise while this is being done, but they rarely if ever desert the nest, as many other species undoubtedly would do.

It is understandable that the Cockatiel, being so popular in Europe, also gained enthusiastic fans in the United States. In fact, it is safe to assume that at the turn of the century Cockatiels were also harbored in American homes and gardens; unfortunately, there are no documents to give definite credence to this assumption.

However, it is specifically the Cockatiel that in recent years has captured American hearts; I am familiar with both the European and American bird markets, and I can confidently state that at the moment there is a considerably larger number of Cockatiel fanciers in the United States than in Europe.

It is a great pity that the average American aviculturist is not conscientious enough, nor does he take color mutations as seriously as he should. I must add, in all fairness, that it is often exactly those Cockatiels that come from American aviaries that surpass the European-bred birds for health and size. Interestingly, the first mutation also came from the United States.

When Gould returned to England in 1840 it probably never occurred to him that the Cockatiel would claim such wide-spread affection. Already back in 1846 in the famous *Jardin des Plantes* in Paris, France, Cockatiel couples were on display for the public, and it goes without saying that breeding results certainly must have been achieved, although we have no records of successful first broods. In 1850 the Cockatiel was successfully bred in Hamburg and Frankfurt, Germany and 13 years later in the London Zoo. In 1865 the first successful brood was registered in the Netherlands, in 1870 in Belgium, in 1881 in Switzerland, in 1900 in India, in 1910 in the United States and in Japan in 1920. It is no wonder that the Cockatiel has gained such world-wide popularity, America and South Africa clearly being at the top. Cockatiels adjust admirably to climate and captivity, and although we no longer receive imports from Australia, their land of origin, bird fanciers from all over the world have the breeding well under control. Consequently, anyone who would like to take this hobby seriously, can choose from a large selection of beautiful birds, or even start with one pair and breed them himself.

Cockatiels do not need to be housed with their own species exclusively. Their nature is such that even Budgerigars or slightly larger finch species can be confidently placed in the same aviary.

The Cockatiel *(Nymphicus hollandicus)* and the Science of Taxonomy

The English alternative name "Cockatoo Parrot" already suggests that the Cockatiel presents a taxonomic problem. Over the years, scientists indeed have discussed widely what the correct name should be. Discussions were held as to the relationship that the Cockatiel might have with other types of birds, especially with Cockatoos on the one hand and the Rosella species (*Platycercus*) on the other. I will not go into the tiring details of theoretical discussions on classification; but to get a better understanding of the Cockatiel, I believe some reference to this aspect would not be a needless exercise. This chapter does not claim to be exhaustive on this topic, of course, and readers who have no interest in classification can safely skip this paragraph. Still, in a monograph about the Cockatiel, the author ought to at least present a passing reference to this extremely interesting subject.

Let me state at the start that I, like many other ornithologists before me, am very strongly inclined to place the Cockatiel in a separate genus: *Nymphicus,* Wagler, because I must join others in admitting up front that there is a close relationship between the Cockatiel and the Cockatoos of the genus *Callocephalon* and *Calyptorhynchus,* judging by the feather pattern. For your reference, let me state here that the first named genus includes the famous Gang-Gang Cockatoo (*Callocephalon fimbriatum*) from southeast Australia, the male version of which is marked with a red crest and crown. (The rest of its feathering is dark grey with light feather margins.) The second group, *Calyptorynchus,* the genus of the Black Cockatoos, comprises first of all the Glossy Cockatoo (*C. lathami*) and the Red-tailed Cockatoo (*C. magnificus*) with its four subspecies (*C. m. magnificus, C m. macrorhynchus, C. m. samueli* and *C. m. nasa*). Then, it also includes, of course, the Black Cockatoo (*C. funereus*) with two subspecies, *C. f. funereus* and *C. f. baudinii.* The Black Cockatoo occurs in southeast and southwest Australia, the Glossy Cockatoo, in eastern Australia, and the Red-tailed Cockatoo, in large parts of eastern, northern, and western Australia—although there is another, relatively small area in the extreme southeast where this species is found.

The name, Cockatoo Parrot, does not appear strange in any way, considering the peaked crest, formed by narrow feathers, the thin cere covering the beak root (which is feathered under the nostrils), the striking cheek patches, and the fact that the male takes part in the brooding procedure. Certainly, these four characteristics can also be found among representatives of both Cockatoo genera mentioned above.

With these facts in mind, one can say with considerable certainty that the Cockatiel is truly a *real* Cockatoo—one which for reasons which apparently can no longer be established, remained behind in size, and so came to look more like a parakeet than a "true" parrot. It is certainly not uncommon that—within a certain group of animals with related characteristics—there suddenly appear deviant physical forms which in the passage of time did not change further (or hardly so), but continued in existence independently.

29

It certainly could also be the case that the Cockatiel still has a closer relationship to the Rosella species than is commonly believed or can be shown ornithologically. But, it is still possible that in the distant past, the Cockatiel adopted some characteristics of certain Cockatoo genera.

Even the placement of the Cockatiel in the genus *Nymphicus* is not definitive for the reason mentioned above. There are even those who declare that the Cockatiel was at the head of the split which eventually divided the Cockatoos from the Rosella species. If this presumption is correct, it would explain why Cockatiels exhibit characteristics of both Cockatoos and Rosella species.

Cockatiels also strongly resemble Cockatoos in their living habits. The relationship to the Rosella species, however, does cause me problems, personally. There are two references in the literature to crosses with, respectively, the Red-rumped Parrot (*Psephotus haematonotus*) and the Blue-winged Parrot (*Neophema chrysostoma*), but these must be regarded with a great deal of reservation, in my opinion. The first reference has no concrete facts behind it, while the second is supposed to have occurred in the aviary of an Australian aviculturist, a certain Mr. Martin. But it appears that this gentleman was supposed to have more curious crosses in his aviary that seem like wishful thinking. He also is reported to have accomplished crosses of the Rose-ringed Parakeet (*Psittacula k. krameri*) with the Crimson Rosella (*Platycercus elegans*); and of the Australian King Parrot (*Alisterus scapularis*) x Red-rumped Parrot (*Psephotus haematonotus*).

The cross between the Rosella (*Platycercus eximius*) and the Cockatiel, which is mentioned in the literature now and then also is extremely subject to doubt. As far as I know, it has never been repeated, although the opportunity for it exists, since the Rosella is kept in many aviaries. All in all, one can safely conclude that in any case, there is no close relationship between the Cockatiel and the Rosella species, given the dubious and never definitively proven reasoning and evidence.

On the basis of the facts just discussed, it seems realistic to classify the Cockatiel as follows:

KINGDOM: Animalia
PHYLUM: Chordata (Phylum: one of the major kinds of groups used in classifying animals, e.g. phylum Chordata. Consists of one class or a number of similar classes. Phylum is not often used in plant classification, the term, Division being substituted).
CLASS: Aves (Birds)
ORDER: Psittaciformes (Parrots and Allies)
FAMILY: Cacatuidae (Cockatoos)
SUBFAMILY: Nymphicinae
GENUS: Nymphicus, Wagler
SPECIES: (Nymphicus) hollandicus (Kerr)

The English name "Cockatiel" (sometimes abbreviated to "Cocky") is hardly, if ever, used by Australians. I remember that when I visited pet shops in Sydney, Adelaide, Melbourne and Perth, I had to use the term "Quarrion," because they didn't understand "Cockatiel" there. The people "down under," moreover, have a great many names for birds and animals that are an anglicization of names given by the indigenous population. In this connection, I think, for example, of Budgerigar, a modification of the name given by the Aborigines to the overly famous "Budgie" or Parakeet, a name originally spelled Betcherrygah" by John Gould, and "Budgerygah" by Dr. J. A. Leach. The term really means "good food" or "pretty bird," two meanings which are synonymous, at least to the Aborigines!

Similarly, I noticed that in large parts of western Australia, the Cockatiel was called "Weero," "Weelarra," "Wamba," "Bula-doota," "Toorir," and "Woo-raling."

Speaking of names, I want to add a few foreign appellations to facilitate any future correspondence, although, of course, use of the scientific name, *Nymphicus hollandicus,* can eliminate all confusion. This scientific name, by the way, is a series of Latin words:

Nymphicus = resembling a nymph
hollandicus = native of Holland, which is the old name for Australia.

A few foreign names are:
Dutch: *Valkparkiet*
French: *Peruche Calopsitte*
German: *Nymphensittich*
Hungarian: *Nimfapapagaj.*

Psittacines is a collective term including among others: macaws, cockatoos, parrots, parakeets, lories, and lovebirds. One can safely say that they have been throughout the ages among the most popular types of birds. The Australasian avifauna includes 45 genera, 150 species, and 298 subspecies. Forshaw (1973) lists—in addition to the subfamily *Nymphicinae* with its single genus containing the Cockatiel—the subfamily *Cacatuinae* with 17 genera, 28 species, 28 subspecies. Altogether Forshaw recognizes within the order *Psittaciformes* 77 genera, 325 species, and 594 subspecies.

Each species, including the Cockatiel of course, is given its own scientific name, as we have already observed. A scientific name is usually built up from Latin and Greek words and constructions, and is uniformly accepted throughout the world. When I correspond with a Chinese and I don't know the Chinese word for the Cockatiel, then I can cite the scientific name, so that misunderstanding is completely ruled out. We both know exactly what we are discussing.

Each scientific name consists of two words such as:
1. *Nymphicus* and
2. *hollandicus.*

The first name is always written with an initial capital, the second without capitalization. Printed in a book or article, the scientific name is consistently printed in italics. The first name gives the name of the genus (*Nymphicus*) and the second, the species (*hollandicus*). A genus comprises a group of similar, related species. Thus, it is quite possible to have a genus with more than a single species.

For example: the Red-tailed Cockatoo, which I mentioned earlier will illustrate. This species has the scientific name *Calyptorhynchus* (= genus) *magnificus* (= species). The bird, however, has some four subspecies, which vary somewhat from the standard form in appearance, habits, habitat, or some other trait. Still, they don't vary enough to recognize them as independent species. Because they are so closely related, these subspecies maintain the first two names, but get a third name to distinguish them from the standard form: *Calyptorhynchus magnificus samueli* or *Calyptorhynchus magnificus nasa.* When making continued references to such subspecies, one spells out the name completely only at the first mention, and after that, one refers to *C.m. samueli* or *C.m. nasa.*

The Cockatiel has no recognized subspecies. Obviously, very closely related genera (plural of genus) are included in one and the same family. Thus, the Black Cockatoo of the genus *Calyptorhynchus,* the White

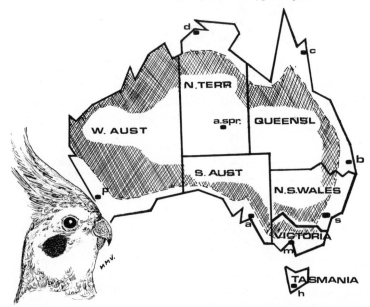

The Cockatiel *(Nymphicus hollandicus)* **is widely distributed throughout the Australian continent, but population density is greater in the interior sections.**
Drawing by the author

Cockatoo of the genus *Cacatua,* and the Pygmy Parrots of the genus *Micropsitta* all belong to the family *Cacatuidae.* Eleven species of that genus appear in Australia, the rest on the islands to the north of Australia.

The scientific classification of plants and animals is called *taxonomy,* and those who busy themselves with this specialty are called *taxonomists.* It is a fact that these scientists don't always see everything the same way. There is some difference of opinion over the number of species, genera, and families that are to be differentiated among the parrots.

The Amazon Parrots provide a clear example:

Forshaw (1973/78)	Wolters (1975)	de Grahl (1974)	Low (1980)
1 *collaria*	*festiva*	*collaria*	*agilis*
2 *leucocephala*	*tucumana*	*leucocephala*	*collaria*
3 *ventralis*	*pretrei*	*ventralis*	*leucocephala*
4 *albifrons*	*agilis*	*xantholora*	*ventralis*
5 *xantholora*	*vittata*	*albifrons*	*albifrons*[3]
6 *agilis*	*albifrons*	*agilis*	*vittata*
7 *vittata*	*xantholora*	*vittata*	*pretrei*[2]
8 *tucumana*	*ventralis*	*pretrei*[2]	*viridigenalis*
9 *pretrei*	*leucocephala*	*viridigenalis*	*finschi*
10 *viridigenalis*	*collaria*	*finschi*	*autumnalis*
11 *finschi*	*xanthops*	*autumnalis*	*dufresniana*
12 *autumnalis*	*finschi*	*dufresniana*	*brasilienis*
13 *brasiliensis*	*viridigenalis*	*brasiliensis*	*festiva*
14 *dufresniana*	*autumnalis*	*arausiaca*	*xanthops*
15 *festiva*	*brasiliensis*	*festiva*	*barbadensis*
16 *xanthops*	*dufresniana*	*xanthops*	*aestiva*
17 *barbadensis*	*mercenaria*	*barbadensis*	*amazonica*
18 *aestiva*	*amazonica*	*aestiva*	*ochrocephala*
19 *ochrocephala*	*barbadensis*	*ochrocephala*	*mercenaria*
20 *amazonica*	*aestiva*	*amazonica*	*farinosa*
21 *mercenaria*	*ochrocephala*	*mercenaria*	*vinacea*
22 *farinosa*	*farinosa*	*farinosa*	*guildingii*
23 *vinacea*	*arausiaca*	*vinacea*	*versicolor*
24 *versicolor*	*versicolor*	*guildingii*	*imperialis*
25 *arausiaca*	*guildingii*	*versicolor*	*arausiaca*
26 *guildingii*	*martinica†*	*imperialis*	[1]
27 *imperialis*	*imperialis*	[1]	[1]
28 [1]	*violacea†*	[1]	
29 [1]	*vinacea*		

[1] = extinct species omitted
[2] = includes *tacumana*
[3] = includes *xantholora*
† = extinct

In light of the above, let us take a closer look at the taxonomic status of the Cockatiel.

33

I have already indicated that the Cockatiel occupies its own category, with apparently a close relationship to some Cockatoo genera. It remains a fact, however, that the feathering of the Cockatiel can be called truly unique, because the combination of the colors gray, white, and yellow can not be found on any other Cockatoo, nor even on any parrot or parakeet whatsoever. Further, one can state firmly in this connection that gray coloration is absent in all other Australian psittacids and Lories. On the other hand, gray is to be found in several Cockatoos, like the Gang-Gang Cockatoo (*Callocephalon fimbriatum*) or the Rose-breasted Cockatoo (*Eolophus roseicapillus*). It also is interesting to note in this respect that several Cockatoos exhibit gray color in their infant feathering. Several White Cockatoos, such as the Sulphur-crested Cockatoo (*Cacatua galerita*), serve as good examples of this.

The cheek pattern and the small, pale stripes in the feathering of young Cockatiels and females also can be found once again in the feathering of some representatives of the genus *Calyptorhynchus* (Black Cockatoos). This pattern is absent in all Australian parrots and Lories.

I just made reference to the Sulphur-crested Cockatoo because this bird also has well defined yellow cheeks and ear coverts, which are so clearly characteristic of Cockatiels. Furthermore, there also are several White Cockatoos that have such cheeks, which leads me to believe there is a relationship between the genera *Nymphicus* and *Calyptorhynchus*. A look at nestlings shows us further additional unmistakable elements in common with Cockatoos. They, like young Cockatiels, are sparsely covered with long, yellow down. Only the Rose-breasted Cockatoo (*Eolophus roseicapillus*) and the White-tailed Cockatoo (*Calyptorhynchus funereus baudinii*), a subspecies of the Black Cockatoo (*C. funereus*), are clear exceptions, and have pink and white down, respectively. As far as the other Australian parrots are concerned, one can state generally that the young have white or gray down, which is, however, replaced rather quickly by a second and relatively thick downy layer, totally masking the bird's skin. The nestlings of Cockatoos and Cockatiels, in contrast, have only a very thin layer of natal down, through which the skin can be distinguished quite clearly. The feathers appear immediately after this downy layer. A second layer of down, which appears in psittacids and Lorikeets, is thus absent in Cockatoos as well as Cockatiels.

Until now, we haven't made much reference to the characteristic crest of the Cockatiel. There is a single, notably unrelated bird, which has a crest similar to that of the Cockatiel, namely the Horned Parakeet (*Eunymphicus cornutus*). (Note the parallelism in the scientific name of the species!). This bird, which appears in New Caledonia and Ouvea (Loyalty Islands) is, however, unable to raise its crest. Cockatoos and Cockatiels do have this ability, and in this trait the strong resemblance of these two genera can again be compared. Further, it is interesting to

34

note that the crest of the Horned Parakeet is a perfect example of convergence, which means that this characteristic trait developed independently in more than one evolutionary line.

Another similarity of Cockatoos and Cockatiels is that neither have a clear courtship display. A very good example of this is courtship feeding of the female. Only the genus *Calyptorhynchus* represents a clearcut exception to this.

Research, furthermore, has established that, among nearly all Australian parrots, only the female broods the eggs and that the male feeds her on the nest. In Cockatiels, both sexes participate in brooding, and this characteristic is shared by all Cockatoos, again with the exception of the genus *Calyptorhynchus*. The Black Cockatoos clearly have a specialization of tasks: the male feeds the female on the nest while she hatches the eggs.

Also in certain patterns of behavior we see further strong parallels between Cockatiels and Cockatoos. Especially in the event of immediate danger, the reactions to threat are strikingly similar. The birds press themselves against the ground or against a thick tree branch (in a low crouch), while softly rocking from left to right. During this movement, they raise the forward parts of their wings, while the wingtips are pressed against the body. In addition, they spread their tail like a fan and they exhale with a hiss through a wide-open beak. Cockatoos and Cockatiels exhibit the same type of behavior when one goes to check on the young in the nest or when they are threatened there by an enemy. In contrast, the reaction of Lorikeets and Australian psittacids is a continuous screeching sound.

Further, note the hoarse begging cry of hungry Cockatiel nestlings, involving vigorous head jerks, when the young accept regurgitated food from the parents. After swallowing the food, the young quiet down completely for a moment, after which they resume their begging cry again. There is no trace of any of this among Australian parrots; it is another unique trait to Cockatoos and Cockatiels.

There are still more parallels: "The sequence of molt of the primary wing feathers, the occurrence of twin patches of powder down on the lumbar region, and a display seen frequently in adult birds which consists of suddenly sweeping the wings forward over the head while perching or standing on the ground." (Allen & Allen, 1978).

Clearly, it's nearly impossible that so many parallel characteristics could have developed independently in the Cockatiels, so that in every way it seems justified to place these birds in *Cacatuidae* (Courtney, 1974).

Of course, there remain some characteristic traits which are *not* shared with the Cockatoos. The most obvious of these is size, of course. No known Cockatoos are as small as Cockatiels, or smaller. Further, Cockatiels have a linear stripe under the wing and noticeably narrow, pointed wings and tail. Also, their flight differs from that of the Cocka-

35

toos. As Forshaw noted, their flight is "swift and direct, the backward-swept pointed wings being moved with deliberate, rhythmic motion; the white wing-patches are very obvious."

Also one could mention the shape of the eggs, the short incubation period, the remarkably short stay of baby birds in the nest, the nodding gesture of the head when they beg for food—which ought not to be confused, by the way, with the feeding jerks that were mentioned above. Further, one could point to the construction of the pineal body and the manner in which the head is scratched. Nonetheless, it ought to be clear to the reader that these dissimilar characteristics dissolve into insignificance if we compare them with traits that do correspond with those of the Cockatoos. In this vein, Holyoak (1972) correctly attaches no great significance to the fact that the Cockatiel scratches its head by raising a leg *over* rather than *under* the wing, which is the way of most Cockatoos. After all, this is a converging characteristic which is shared by a great number of parrots that forage mainly on the ground.

In this connection, I must point out, that Cockatiels *do* use a leg for eating, even though this is uncommon, a fact that Holyoak and Courtney don't seem to accept. An extensive study including wild birds as well as birds in cages and aviaries brought me face to face several times with Cockatiels that hold their food with their legs.

Nonetheless, one can state, in general terms, that the Cockatiel's feed selection and flight pattern show more correspondence with Platycercines (Rosella species) than with Cockatoos. But these two traits seem more evolutionary than phylogenetic, or as Allen and Allen say: ". . . . the non-cacatuid characters which are related to body shape (i.e., wings and tail) and feeding behavior probably represent adaptions to a particular habitat. Some of the Platycercine parrots exploit this same habitat in a fashion similar to the Cockatiel and a certain degree of convergence between the two is not surprising."

The Wild Cockatiel

The wild Cockatiel (*Nymphicus hollandicus*) is, together with the Budgerigar (*Melopsittacus undulatus*) the most common Australian bird species to be found. He has an extremely slim and quick appearance and is approximately 12 inches long. As can be seen on a map, the Cockatiel populates practically all of Australia, the smallest continent, with the exception of the coastal areas of the north, east, south and partly the west. In Tasmania the Cockatiel is usually not to be found (we will refer to this later on), which, however, may be considered somewhat strange, in view of the fact that he is an extremely skillful flyer and could easily bridge a relatively small distance. From the Cockatiel no geographical under-species are to be distinguished, though it may rightly be said that especially

36

the male Cockatiels of Queensland are shaded strikingly deeper, than the rest of the Australian Cockatiels.

A full grown male Cockatiel is mainly grayish-brown; the rump and the upper tail coverts have a somewhat silvery glow. The under surface of the tail-feathers is black. The slim, strongly muscled wings are a dark gray, with nearly black or black shades at the top of the flight feathers.

The Cockatiel is, of course, immediately characterized by its yellow crested head. The crest generally stands upright, but can also be flattened. This, however, is seldom done: contrary to the crest of Cockatoo, which serves as an excellent indicator of the bird's mood. The orange-red cheeks and ear-coverings of the Cockatiel are also characteristic of this bird.

The crest has a lemon shade and the iris of the eye is dark brown. The median wing coverts and the great wing coverts are white. Therefore, it appears as if the bird has a partly white shoulder and wing.

Beak and legs are slate gray.

The adult hen is immediately distinguishable from the male; she is of a noticeably fainter shade and marking, especially on the head, which is significantly grayer. At any rate the wavy, yellow banded underside of the tail is quite characteristic for the hen. Lendon indicates that: "Cockatiels exhibit a variation of the wing-stripe of the broadtails. It consists of four or five yellowish spots on the inner webs of both the primaries and secondaries and is present in the adult female and in the immature of both sexes, but is lost in the adult male."

Young Cockatiels look very much like the hen, and as yet it is very difficult to color-distinguish the sexes. At about six months the young males get the lemon-yellow head, but it takes another six months before they are fully colored and can no longer be distinguished from mature adults.

Cockatiels live in pairs, in small groups of from four to 12 birds. Sometimes larger groups of up to several hundred occur. Because they spend most of their time on the ground, it could at once be supposed that Cockatiels can be found exclusively in open areas. This is, however, only partly true. In Adelaide, the capital city of South Australia, I observed, throughout the year, various Cockatiels in the so-called "parklands": large grass fields with some scattered groups of trees (often under which park benches are situated) which are three times and more the size of a football field. I have often spotted signs of them in the rather dense forest areas, as well as (as one might expect) on the open savannas. The view here is partly unhampered. After the rainy season the grasses grow rather tall and their movement can be a signal to potential enemies. For this reason Cockatiels routinely fly upward as their quick flight is their best defense. The birds usually fly to their own territory or lookout positions, generally a thick branch of an old leafless tree.

Cockatiels in general are likely to be found in places located not far from fresh water, where they drink in the morning and (especially) in the evening. They do this quickly and skillfully. Yet it is definitely stated that Cockatiels can live without water for some time, provided they have no need to cover long and tiring distances; the birds seem to obtain sufficient fluids, necessary for maintaining health, from seeds and other food sources.

Cockatiels often wander from one feeding ground to another; they are clearly nomadic in northern Australia, and more or less migrant in the south. Only during the breeding season when their habitat offers more than sufficient food through the ripening grasses, do the birds stay in one area, as well as foraging a surprisingly long distance away. They can remain in a (for them) favorable habitat for some time and even raise several broods there. Because of the natural growth of the group, through the youngsters, the food-sources naturally become scarcer. Diminished food sources force the young birds to leave their parents and live elsewhere. If the parents still have a brood, previously-born young depart, especially to areas situated nearer the coast. Thus, in this way Cockatiels may be sighted at locations previously unknown for the species. It is also evident that the total population encroaches more and more toward the coastal areas.

According to Loeding (1979) such "migrating" young birds are presently even being sighted in Tasmania; this was also stated by Dr. Immelmann in 1962, and myself in 1964, and so this is by no means a present-day phenomenon.

I also learned from different sources that especially over the last few years, young Cockatiels are being sighted regularly in the eucalyptus woods around Bridgetown, in the Australian southwest.

However, it is a fact that most of the young birds from Tasmania, as well as those from the so-called eucalyptus woods, again return to the general vicinity of their birthplace after from one to three months; to date it is a rather unique occurrence when the young birds decide to settle in the new area and begin breeding. If they do, new populations come into existence which finally results in the enhanced survival of the species. Naturally this is an extremely important and highly desirable circumstance.

Basically it can be stated then that the Cockatiel encroaches more and more towards coastal areas. This has come about because of the arid inland, which is becoming drier and where evidently a warmer climate is developing, and where water will gradually become scarce. The over-cropping committed by man on the forested biota has also forced the birds away from interior regions.

The Cockatiel is easily the fastest flyer among the parrots and Budgerigars of Australia. The bird's torpedo-shaped body and the long, slim, well-muscled wings make this possible. When a Cockatiel flies over at a high level, with quick, elegant, and effortless flight, it describes an almost completely straight line. Sometimes surprising distances are covered to obtain food, and often this occurs from one regular area which is both a departure and arrival spot. When the bird decides to return to the ground to continue foraging, the path of descent is a perpendicular line and is again extremely quick and skillful. It seems as if the bird falls like a stone from heaven; only some yards above the ground will the tail and wings be spread—like the brake flaps of a plane-wing.

Immelman states that the white wingstripe is probably a good distinguishing mark to keep birds of a certain group together. During flight, or while the flock is eating, a soft, continual sound like "quil-quil," can be heard. When the birds fly over low, the yellow head of the male or the yellow tail of the hen may be distinctly observed.

Although Cockatiels forage on the ground for the greater part of the day, they really cannot be considered ground dwellers. They will also look for tidbits, such as seeds, blossoms, nectar and insects in shrubs and trees. When looking for food on the ground, they will also fly up regularly to survey their surroundings.

Because of their color they are very difficult for predators to see, though even while eating they are not quiet and their continuous babbling attracts attention. As a result, over-flying Cockatiels and other birds are often attracted as well and so join the foraging group on the ground.

When Cockatiels detect a suspicious sound, they immediately take flight, settling on the previously-mentioned viewing post in a tree. When, after a thorough investigation, everything is considered safe again, they return to the ground. If indeed there is a genuine threat, they quickly fly away.

At drinking areas they are extremely timid and alert. Before drinking, they will circle many times above the water and along the banks, to ascertain that all is safe. Then they land in their typical quick way and come down in shallow water. I have never seen Cockatiels stand at river-banks to quench their thirst. After some hasty sips they fly up again, circle for some time above the water, and go down again to drink. Sometimes I saw birds taking a few quick sips, and within a few seconds (you are reading correctly!) disappear again; another time they would fly away immediately after arrival—for reasons unknown to me, but undoubtedly some danger threatened—so they fled without having had a drink.

Furthermore, Cockatiels very much like a rain bath; many times I saw them thoroughly enjoying themselves in the spray of a lawn-sprinkler or in the sprinklers of the parklands in Adelaide, Perth and Melbourne.

In connection with this I would like to cite Dr. George A. Smith (from: *Encyclopedia of Cockatiels,* Copyright © 1978, TFH Publications):

As rain starts to fall, and most especially after a dry spell, the Cockatiels will fly around in an ecstasy of excitement, giving their flight call of *weel, weel.* They perch with the wings and tail spread wide to catch the falling drops and hang upside down to wet the few remaining dry areas of the body. This fluttering and posturing and shrieking has all the wild, excited abandon of young children who, out of sight of the parents, have found for themselves a nice muddy puddle to splash in. Once the Cockatiels are sopping wet they sit drying and preen themselves and their partners' heads. The excitement of flying and posturing usually sets off the males into a frenzy of sexual display. They sing to their hens and give the *wher-wetit whew* and *were-it, were-it, were-it* calls. The calling begins slowly and gradually increases to a tempo. The male also starts to search for nesting holes, accompanied by his "wife." If the rain continues long enough, this daily activity starts the pair nesting in earnest.

It seems that adult Cockatiels remain paired throughout most of the year. When the opportunity to breed does come they do not have to frantically search for a mate and then undertake a rapid courtship. The permanent bond between a mated pair is strengthened not only by mutual head-preening and close attendance one upon the other, but also by copulation. Pairing may take place several times a day except for when they are molting. The hen can lay fertile eggs within about four days of the pair finding a suitable cavity in which to lay, the ovaries being in a state of full development for most of the year.

Cockatiels feel most at east when they can observe the surroundings for possible danger through the branches of the eucalyptus tree, and indeed there they are barely noticeable. The gray bark of the eucalyptus with the white spots (where the bark has come off) offers excellent camouflage and thus perfect protection. As a matter of fact, the birds seem to be conscious of this as they will let humans and animals approach to within a few yards of their look-out perch. Most birds I observed in this manner were sitting lengthwise on the branches, instead of across them. These branches certainly need not be full of leaves, as even in leafless trees we found Cockatiels! Talk about "being sure of their position!"

Through banding bird couples it has become apparent that Cockatiels will, at least for the duration of one breeding season, remain together; Dr. Smith found this to be true also. Outside the breeding period—as previously mentioned—they generally operate in small groups, and it is not altogether clear whether the pairs display any special attention to each other. In such groups we also often find Budgerigars, and I noticed, most evidently, that they are certainly not timid and frequently more impertinent and savage than the Cockatiels. Cockatiels probably preen each other in the wild state as well as in captivity. They are less active during the breeding period and I can personally agree with Dr. Lendon, as I have observed similar cases in the south and east of Australia.

The whole occurrence of breeding is attuned to the rainy season. In the south of Australia this is in springtime, which means during the months of August-December. In the north of their habitat the breeding takes place more or less towards the end of the rainy season which includes the months of April-June. In this period the grass and weeds are in full bloom, and

40

as seeds are the most important part of their diet, it is clear that in this period the young are brought up. Further, all sorts of trees are also in bloom, which produce nectar and blossoms and provide insects, small snails and spiders. In central Australia the breeding season occurs during any favorable month of the year. Even *during* the rainy season I observed enthusiastic pairs with young.

Lendon states that he once saw how a new Cockatiel hen was placed with a male; the courting-dance consisted of a series of somewhat comical small leaps by the male as he was pertly running after her; meanwhile emitting a low sounding variant of the normal shrill call. Curlews in love— just think of the Budgerigars—feeding each other from the crop. I have never seen this with Cockatiels, not in the wild state, nor in captivity.

The Cockatiel's nest is usually found in a hole or hollow of a thick, moldy branch or trunk of a dead tree. It struck me that all the wild nests I found were always situated extremely strategically, thus the breeding bird was at all times able to look around for any possible danger while it was still far away. Furthermore Cockatiels do not object to breeding in trees where Budgerigars and Cockatoos are also raising their families; I frequently found several Budgies' nests in one and the same tree as well.

Usually the clutch consists of four to five eggs; in general it is rather rare when six to nine eggs are produced. The eggs are strikingly round, white and measure 1" x ¾" (24.5 x 19.0 mm) (Forshaw). They are laid in a thin layer of moldy wood which serves as a small "delivery-bed" on the bottom of the hollow. Usually, the first egg is laid four days after copulation.

As with some Cockatoos, Cockatiels take turns with brooding. There is, however, a clear sharing of the work: the male will brood during the day, while the hen sits on the eggs during the afternoon and night. At night the male remains near the nest taking light naps. At the slightest suspicious sound his head goes up like a hot-tempered Bantam cock's, in order to locate the danger. It has also been frequently observed that a Cockatiel, before returning to the nest to brood, will first take an extensive bath, no doubt to slightly moisten the nest. This moistening will certainly further the incubation of the eggs, because in this way the egg membrane will not dry out (which would make it hard and tough). This will also enable the youngsters to free themselves from the egg more easily.

In his rich, to our taste somewhat exaggerated prose, Dr. W. T. Greene says in *Parrots in Captivity* (1884-1887) reprinted by TFH Publications, 1979:

Like all the Parrot tribe, the Cockatiel makes its nest in the hollow bough of a tree, where it lays a considerable number of eggs, seldom less than five, often seven, and not infrequently nine [here Greene is not quite correct, M.M.V.], which it hatches in twenty-one days from the date of the deposition of the last of the batch. The male is a most attentive father, sitting on the eggs all day, from five or six o'clock in the morning, during summer, to four or five in the evening, seldom leaving them for more than a few minutes occasionally to get a little food; but when he thinks he has done his duty he comes off, and if the hen, as sometimes happens, appears unwilling to take up her position in the nest, a grand scolding takes place, and now and then a regular fight. "It is too bad!" he screams, "there, I have been sitting all day, and you have been out enjoying yourself in the sunshine, and now, when I am faint and hungry, and the daylight almost gone, you will not do your duty, but let the precious eggs get cold! It is too bad I declare, go in at once, o wife, go in I say!" And if madame does not at once take up her post on the eggs, he chases her about, pecking her sharply and scolding vehemently all the time; until at last, fatigued by his importunities, if not obeying the call of duty, she pops into the box, settles herself down on her eggs, and he, giving a congratulatory chuckle, flies off to the seed-pan, and makes up for the lost time by eating voraciously for several minutes, when he repairs to the water-bottle and has a good drink, then he plumes himself for a little while, and then it is time to go to bed.

Of course, any comment on my part would be unbecoming!

After a breeding period of about 21 days the eggs will hatch; the young have cream colored down and pale yellow beaks. They are fed by both parent birds for about four to five weeks. Also, when the youngsters have left their breeding nest, their parents continue to provide tidbits for another two to three weeks. After that period, however, they can be considered to be independent. Their food consists mainly of ripe as well as unripe grass —and weed seeds.

We can observe Cockatiels in the blossoming eucalyptus trees where they enjoy the nectar and probably small insects and other animal food. They also like to dwell in areas where wheat is grown and the damage they may cause there can be considered small. Yet flocks of approximately 200 birds are often observed during that time.

At one time Australian farmers poisoned drinking areas or scattered poisoned seeds around their fields. Not only Cockatiels, but many other birds and mammals died as a result. Fortunately such practices do not occur any more or only to a very small extent; through modern technique (for instance, by sounding the birds' cries of alarm through means of loud-speakers), more effective defenses have been invented, without disturbing Nature itself.

Nevertheless, in several Australian states it is permissible to shoot Cockatiels during certain seasons; in other states, as in New South Wales, the Cockatiel is legally protected.

As it is, Cockatiels are nevertheless exposed to new dangers, owing to our modern technology. In fact every year traffic claims many, many victims—human and animal!

I already mentioned that Cockatiels may be frequently seen in the parklands, close to populated areas, and even within such areas. Many times I have observed small victims of traffic, together with other Parakeets and Cockatoos. Fortunately, thanks to their extremely quick and skillful flight, most Cockatiels manage to escape this disaster, or as Greene says:

Although good walkers and quick runners, the Cockatiels are also strong on the wing, and circle round and round their domicile, in a bold and graceful manner, when let out for a fly: this is an accomplishment they learn quickly, but had better be taught in the country than in London, where such multitudes of cats are ever on the lookout for a morsel, and have no more scruple in pouncing on the most valuable exotic bird that, unfortunately, falls in their way, than on the dirtiest and most disreputable of cockney sparrows.

"Now where did that cat go?"   *Courtesy Ruth Hanessian*

3

The Cockatiel as a Pet

So it all depends on whether your love for birds and the joy you get out of breeding them and watching them raise their cute babies means enough to you to sacrifice your house, or at least one room of your house. And if not, it would be best to have a male bird only. Of course, a hen makes just as sweet a pet, but the male can talk and whistle. And when you are not loving and playing with him or watching his antics, he can be kept in a smaller cage with less harm than the laying breeding hen.

Mrs. E. L. Moon in
Experiences with my Cockatiels
(Copyright © 1976, TFH Publications)

WHEN A PROSPECTIVE AVICULTURIST first decides to buy birds, he rarely realizes that a sensible purchase is the decisive factor for a gratifying start.

Usually the new hobbyist discovers, for instance, beautiful pied Cockatiels, and sets his heart on them. The buyer has no idea what these birds, as a rule, have been through before finally reaching a shop. They may have had a long, exhausting journey, having found their way to the pet shop via a distributor and sometimes even through a middleman.

During this "voyage," the birds have been confined to a small cage, sometimes with hundreds of fellow-sufferers, and have had to adapt to a different diet and to entirely different surroundings. This is why a sensible bird

45

dealer will put all of his new arrivals into a spacious aviary and see to it that they get absolute rest for the first few days, as well as a balanced diet.

No matter where the birds come from, it is absolutely essential that they have a chance to adapt.

Selecting and Purchasing Pet Birds

It is understandable that the purchase is a matter requiring considerable thought. If, for instance your special interest is breeding Cockatiels, buy them in early spring or at the very beginning of fall so that the temperature is in their favor from the very first.

We place our newcomers in large cages for at least two weeks, where there are no drafts and plenty of light. We feed the birds the same kind of food they had before arriving at our house, in addition to such food as we know to be essential for their well-being. The food at the majority of the pet stores is usually restricted to some mixed seeds or a commercial mixture. Your new birds are certain not to have known a wide variety, which is why it is so important for the aviculturist to know exactly what food the birds actually need before even setting out to buy them.

As no bird, generally speaking, can go without food for more than 24 hours, it is essential to buy only those birds which can be transported to their destination—your home—preferably within a couple of hours. The shorter the trip, the better it will be for the birds. Should you be obliged to put newcomers in their cages for the first time at night, leave the lights on for a couple of hours to allow the birds to eat and to drink as required.

It is also advisable not to leave the birds in total darkness for the first few days; have a small light on for them so they can get used to their surroundings and do not have to fly around in the dark, which could have very unpleasant consequences; serious injuries are often caused when the birds collide with bars or wire netting.

Don't forget to spread some food on the bottom of the cages and aviaries, as well as in the different feeding cups; few young birds are used to the various food receptacles and will instinctively look for food on the bottom of the cage or aviary. Birds have died of starvation because there was no food on the floor, when all the time the Cockatiel had been almost sitting on its feeding cup, with all of the food it needed!

Another thing to observe closely for the first few days is the condition of the Cockatiel's droppings, which should not be watery. If they are, it is advisable to move the bird to warmer surroundings, such as a small "hospital cage" where an even temperature of 86°-94° F (30°-35° C) can be maintained.

However, don't start treating the patient immediately; it is sufficient at first to feed it a little bread soaked in milk and at the same time add a few drops of an antibiotic to its drinking water; a few drops of honey on the bread will do wonders. Of course, the bird can't be put back in a larger cage or in the aviary

46

until it is completely cured; this should preferably be done in the morning of a warm, sunny day. In this way the bird has a chance to adapt to its new surroundings and to find its way to food and drink.

Purchasing a Cockatiel has always been a matter of trust. Still, it is wise to first look at the birds in various pet stores or other suppliers and not decide at once.

Never buy a Cockatiel with ruffled feathers, since that usually spells trouble. Always observe the Cockatiels from a little distance; if you stand too close to a cage or aviary full of Cockatiels, they will fly around in panic, making it difficult to pick out the less healthy birds. When a Cockatiel is healthy, its feathers are sleek and close to its body. The bird is constantly looking in all directions, reacting to the actions of other birds; in short, it makes an alert, cheery impression. When you step closer, it takes to its wings at once. If it doesn't—if it stays in the same place—this is a sign that it is coming down with some disease, rather than a sign of tameness. An active bird, once accustomed to its new quarters, will become very tame toward its owner.

Before you decide to buy a Cockatiel, if possible, hold the bird in your hand or get the seller to do it for you. In any case, check the bird's condition to see if it has been properly fed; to do so effectively, you should hold the bird so its back rests against your palm. Now you can check its breast with thumb and forefinger. If the breastbone protrudes sharply, the bird is too thin, which means that its muscles are underdeveloped. Indeed, there is nothing more to check in that case, because Cockatiels in that condition should be avoided. Any properly-fed bird has well-developed muscles at either side of the ridge on its breastbone, and in that case only a slight edge can be felt.

If the Cockatiel is not too thin, one might buy it, provided that the feathers around its vent are clean. When they are soiled, it is a sign that the bird might suffer from intestinal catarrh, a difficult disease to cure. No sale in that case, either.

By the way, don't make a very common mistake. There is one phenomenon that occurs quite frequently and tends to confuse a prospective buyer. A young bird (not hand-reared) will usually be so frightened when picked up that it will produce some watery feces, but this phenomenon has nothing to do with diarrhea or any other form of abdominal disturbance. In itself it is no cause to reject the Cockatiel; it is quite a normal reaction. Once in its new quarters, the bird will soon forget its fright, get accustomed to its owner and display all of its intrinsic charm.

Other minor flaws should give no cause for worry, either; one or more feathers missing, say from tail or wings, or broken tail feathers. These conditions are caused by flying around in cages which are often too small, by transfers from one cage to another, by constant catching, examination and other activities not conducive to the welfare of the Cockatiel's plumage. Good care and housing will soon result in the recovery of damaged or missing

47

feathers. It is also of the utmost importance that one purchase only young birds.

Be wary of exceptionally low prices, since they almost always will indicate that something is wrong. Usually "bargain" birds don't want to or just can't breed, they might be fighters, or something else is wrong. Good birds simply are not cheap, and we certainly ought to beware of "bargains."

Sometimes Cockatiels—especially young ones—have tiny pieces of fruit stuck to their bills. These pieces cause an impediment in the growth of their feathers, and hence, bald spots around the bill. This is not a reason not to buy those birds, since painstaking care will soon cure the problem. Such birds, during their transportation and stay in various places, are fed large chunks of banana, orange, fig, pear and/or other fruits, which stick to the base of their beaks; through insufficient bathing facilities and often too much heat in the housing accommodations, the birds cannot get rid of the chunks of fruit and their feathers cannot grow in these spots. If the birds are fed shredded fruit, the feathers around their beaks will soon grow back.

As Cockatiels are primarily seed-eating birds, the characteristics to look for include a gleaming plumage, bright eyes, healthy legs, nails of reasonable length and well-formed and well-closed beaks. Moreover, their feces shouldn't be watery.

Now the question arises, how many birds are we going to buy? Will we (as beginners) content ourselves with a few birds in a lovely, decorative cage or perhaps a not-too-large aviary? Or, do we have enough room to build a large, outside garden aviary, as discussed elsewhere? Do we only wish to purchase Cockatiels for their colors, their general behavior, or do we intend to let them breed as well?

The most popular form of the bird hobby, surprisingly enough, still appears to be keeping one specimen in a cage, usually a bird that can learn to talk to some extent or that catches the eye with its colors (various mutations).

If you want to breed young birds, either in a birdroom, indoor aviary or garden aviary, you should remember that it is advisable not to place all different species together as some birds can be very aggressive, especially during the mating and the breeding season. That is why it's better not to put too many birds in the same quarters; be selective, don't overdo things. You'll soon notice, through daily or nightly fights and chases, which birds don't match. It goes without saying that the culprits should be housed elsewhere as soon as possible. Incidental squabbles are of no consequence, provided that they aren't really serious.

We do best if we put only those birds in the same quarters that are of approximately the same size and need the same care. Lovebirds (*Agapornidae*) and Cockatiels, by the way, are best kept separately in order to prevent casualties and leg mutilation.

Even among Cockatiels there are some who simply don't live up to what is expected of them, whereas others are extremely peaceful and produce a string of handsome young birds.

48

In order to achieve reasonable breeding results, there are certain points we should observe. In the first place, one should never use Cockatiels for breeding that are too young. Cockatiels should be at least 18-24 months old. That is why, again, it is very important to know the descent, age and conduct of our birds, knowledge which can only be achieved by an excellent administrative system.

The second point to observe concerns efficient housing and a good diet. By efficient housing I mean a space in which the Cockatiels can fly around freely, without being hindered by abundant greenery or too many perches. If you don't have much space available, you will just have to choose a few pairs that are content with less space. An aviary, preferably in the garden, remains the best housing in any case. If you surround the aviary with shrubs and plants, it will not just "stand there," but will blend with the natural spot you have created.

Besides available surface and flying space, your choice of birds is of the utmost importance in an aviary of definite dimensions. It's wise to remember that more seed eaters (such as Cockatiels) can find a place than insect or fruit-eaters (soft-billed birds). If quarrels occur regularly among birds that normally ought to be quite peaceable, that is sufficient evidence that the aviary either has the wrong mix of species or is overpopulated, which calls for quite drastic measures. Such quarrels develop especially around the feeding cups, in sitting and sleeping quarters, nests and so on. Of course, we aren't referring to those normal sham fights that occur in every aviary or cage once in a while, but to the real skirmishes that are fought with wings and beaks.

Once you have placed your Cockatiels in good quarters, you will need to start looking after them. They must have fresh bathing and drinking water daily, sufficient greens (every day), egg-food and conditioning food, a rich assortment of seeds, a slice of bread soaked in water or milk (the latter especially during the breeding season), cuttlefishbone, and so on.

Watch daily for irregularities among the birds, keeping an eye open for possible illness, isolating affected birds at once.

A cage should be given a fresh layer of sand on the bottom at least twice a week; the aviary must be dug up or deeply raked at least every two weeks. Around breeding time this should be omitted for a while, so as not to disturb the breeding couples. Keep everything as clean as possible so that germs don't stand a chance, which means that drinking and bathing cups, sleeping quarters, perches and so on must be cleaned and disinfected regularly. Indeed, you should be prepared to spend at least an hour a day with your birds; otherwise, you might as well forget the whole thing. And don't bite off more than you can chew; start with one pair of Cockatiels.

One more thing—an avid bird enthusiast normally can't tear himself away from his birds, but don't let your family suffer. Your pastime is precisely one ideally suited to help your friends and especially your children get closer to Nature. Take them with you to your aviary, point out the birds' distinctive

49

features, let them hold a couple of nests, eggs and youngsters. You'll soon find out that this way you are raising Nature lovers, and nowadays we need a lot of those!

The Outdoor Aviary

People all too readily think that every cage and every type of aviary, whether indoors or outdoors, is suitable for housing Cockatiels. A golden rule with which everyone should comply (although, unfortunately, in practice people seldom do) is that proper housing should be ready before the birds come. Before paying attention to the birds themselves we shall restrict ourselves to some general remarks which should always be applied, no matter what birds we have and where we are going to house them. It is important that the housing be in good condition before we think of buying birds; these are no empty words but an essential point with which the hobby stands or falls.

The size and type of enclosure of, for instance, a garden aviary is a very personal matter and depends largely upon available space.

We should also pay attention to the fact that birds can either be housed indoors or outdoors. Indoors, people mainly keep (and often even breed) birds in basements and in bedrooms that are not being used.

Naturally occupants of apartments have no other choice. They frequently use an empty room or, if conditions permit, construct a small outdoor aviary on the balcony.

But most bird-lovers prefer aviaries constructed outside in the garden or yard. For nothing is better for our winged friends than "fresh air." The other side of the picture is only too true, however: nothing is worse for birds than draft, mist and polluted air. Consequently many bird lovers find satisfactory solutions by constructing bird accommodations in garages, basements or attics (with the use of skylights). These plans tend to yield very satisfactory results, thanks to the equipment introduced to the market in recent years.

Aviaries should always be built so the front faces *south* or, if this is impossible, *west*.

When constructing an aviary only use the best material to avoid being faced with new expenses in a couple of years when the wire-netting and wooden frame need renewing. With the steady increase in prices, cutting corners will cost you more in the end.

Use thin planks, the thinner the better since they shrink and expand less. For wire-netting, use squarely welded netting which is available in a variety of gauges (0.5 or 0.6 inches are common) at every do-it-yourself or hobby store. First coat the netting with wax and then paint it with lead-free black paint so that the Cockatiels can be viewed more easily. The roof of the aviary will have a second wire-netting (a netting with large mesh) over the first one in order to make it difficult or impossible for any predators to sit on the roof, frightening the aviary's inhabitants to death. We can also span the sides with double wire-

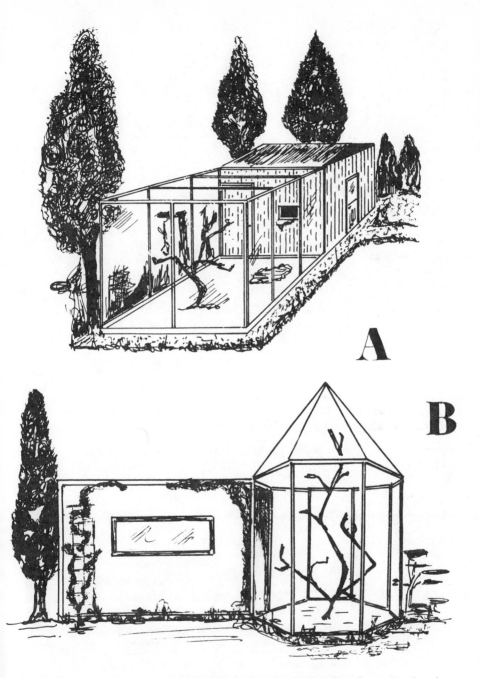

A. This attractive aviary is especially suitable for keeping Cockatiels and some species of small parakeets. B. An octagonal aviary adjoining an enclosed night shelter.

Designs and drawings by the author

This home aviary is located in an area of extreme climatic variation. Therefore it was designed, situated and built to provide birds with maximum comfort in any weather.

Photo by Kelley, from ALL ABOUT THE PARROTS, © 1980 by Arthur Freud, and reproduced with the permission of the publisher, Howell Book House Inc.

A well-designed, self-contained aviary that makes wise use of translucent panels. These admit light and help retain heat, and are sturdier and safer than glass.

Photo by Kelley, from ALL ABOUT THE PARROTS, © 1980 by Arthur Freud, and reproduced with the permission of the publisher, Howell Book House Inc.

netting (of the same type), once again for protection of the inhabitants. The space between the two nettings should be at least four inches. The wisest thing to do is fasten all the netting on the outside of the aviary to avoid injury to the birds, and the risk of catching their bands on a wire-edge. By attaching a wooden strip across the length of the aviary where the netting has been nailed to the wood with staples, it will not only look neater but all the hooks, corners, wire-edges and the like will be covered so as to present no danger to the Cockatiels.

The Shelter

Every good aviary consists of three compartments, i.e. (1) a shelter, (2) an open flight (3) an enclosed flight. It should have one or more windows that are protected by a fine wire mesh. This is to prevent the birds from flying against the windows with a violent smash and thereby injuring themselves badly; in such cases broken wings or legs are very possible.

Guard against rats and mice in every possible way, or better still, do not give any rodents a chance to get to your birds. Anyone who has witnessed the damage and above all the fear that rats cause in an aviary at night will immediately swear an oath: once, but never again. Floors of concrete or heavy paving stones will at least present a difficult task for these predators (although it is known that mice and rats, be it with difficulty of course, can, in fact, gnaw through concrete). If you prefer an earthen floor it is necessary to dig a netting into the ground at the sides of the framework to a depth of 16 to 20 inches. You can, if you like, "bury" fragments of glass, broken bottles and similar rubble, etc., around the aviary at a depth of 16 inches. With a small aviary you can dig up the whole ground to a depth of 16 inches and cover it with wire-netting; then sprinkle sand over it.

With this method natural vegetation is very well possible.

Another way to construct a small aviary is to build the whole aviary on a platform of, say, 12 inches and leave enough room for a dog to crawl underneath it. I would not take the risk of keeping a cat; experience has shown that a dog scares off rats and mice adequately, provided that you have a dog with spirit. Dachshunds or small terriers are good choices.

Poisons are obtainable which destroy rats and mice but are harmless to birds. I would strongly advise against the sprinkling of poison in areas frequented by children.

In addition there would be no sense in pouring concrete when you have actually seen rats and mice around the aviary, since they can easily gnaw another tunnel towards the aviary when the concrete is still soft. But if you keep the aviary clean and regularly clear away the spilled seed that has not been eaten there is not much chance of having mice and rats around. However it is advisable to keep a sharp look-out for these rodents. In this case prevention is better than cure.

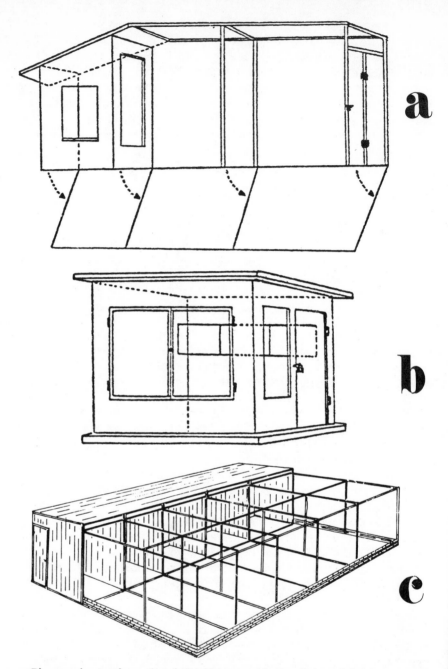

a. Diagram of an outdoor aviary designed as a combination flight and shelter. b. A sensible aviary for use in areas of inhospitable climate. c. This type of aviary is very popular for outdoor use and consists of compartmental shelters and flights (pens).

Designs and drawings by the author

The width of the aviary is not very important as opposed to the length which is of vital importance. The longer the aviary the better. The height presents no major difficulty: however the minimum height should be about six feet. Too high an aviary will obviously cause problems when birst must be caught in preparation for the coming of winter. For a beginner, an aviary of approximately 17 feet long, five feet wide and seven feet high is ideal. If you have set your mind on a breeding aviary with only one pair of Cockatiels the size 10 x 5 x 7 feet will do.

Every aviary (flight) has a roost or shelter that should be bright in order to urge the birds to spend the night in it or to take shelter in it when the weather is bad. It is a well-known fact that most birds like to go to roost as high up as possible. Even when we see to it that the run has lower perches than the shelter, the birds could still accept the shelter as their "bedroom."

With long aviaries it is advisable to cover a part of the flight; this way birds can sit outside and stay dry in rainy weather. Besides, there are many Cockatiels that like to get wet in a soft rain shower; hence a shower can do no harm, especially not in spring and summer.

If, for certain reasons, it is impossible to construct a shelter, then there is the possibility of partially covering one of the extreme points of the run at the top and at the sides with plastic corrugated sheets; this way the birds will still have a safe spot where they can take shelter.

An outdoor aviary with a "porch" is strongly recommended to prevent your birds' attempts to escape.

Unfortunately it is also necessary to lock up the aviary with a secure padlock. You may also want to consider installing an alarm system, since stealing exotic birds has become increasingly common. It is, therefore, wise to band birds and to keep careful records of this. Although it is easy to remove the bands, people are usually suspicious—with reason—when offered birds without bands.

Establish an efficient routine for replenishing food and water. When you choose the right location for eating and drinking utensils, not surrounded by vegetation, it will encourage peace, especially in the breeding season. An ideal approach would be to refill food and water by way of a small door or from the outside, but of course this is not always possible.

The floor of the aviary should be dug up and/or raked regularly, especially after the breeding season. Concrete or tiles can be used for the floor of the aviary. The covered part of the run can, of course, be planted in a natural manner, but the vegetation should be watered regularly. Planting of the shelter can consist of a dead tree with an abundant network of branches; the planting in the outdoor run can of course consist of living trees and bushes. You can also place plants around the aviary in order not to have the aviary stand out in the garden; nothing is more disturbing than this. An aviary should fit in with the layout of the garden, so good vegetation around the aviary is essential.

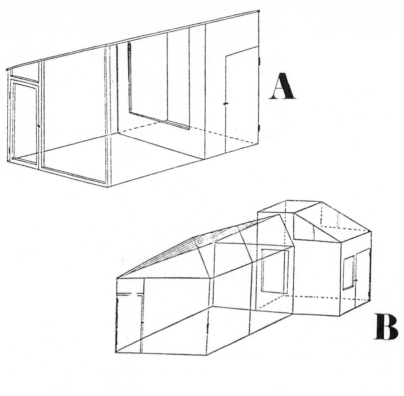

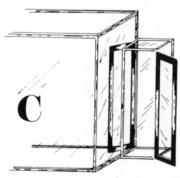

A. A simple, well-constructed garden aviary. B. This aviary is based on the same use as A, but is somewhat more elaborate. C. An aviary porch. The porch attached to an outdoor aviary is an important precaution against the possibility of escape.

Designs and drawings by the author

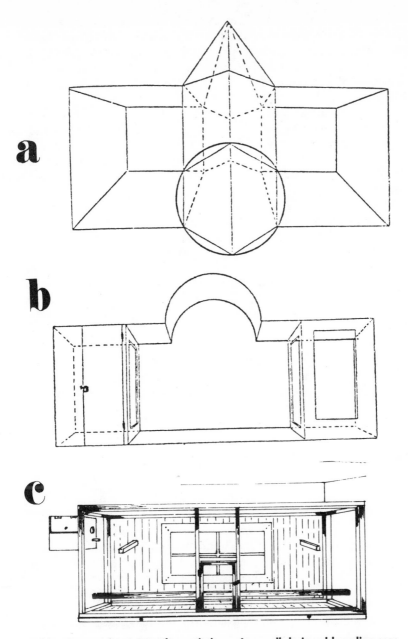

a. and **b.** Diagrams for two outdoor aviaries. **c.** In a well-designed breeding cage the back wall is equipped with a small window in the back wall. This allows for observation of the breeding pair when the cage fronts on a window in the house.

Designs and drawings by the author

In a corner of the aviary, regularly sow some seed; the seed that comes up will be eaten with pleasure by the birds. Another part of the floor could be supplied with a layer of grit which should be replenished regularly.

Always give the birds fresh branches daily (willow, fruit trees, privet and such), as the vegetation is not safe from their destructive beaks that peck at everything.

Let me emphasize a few important facts:

If you intend to breed Cockatiels, you will need aviary facilities. It is best to construct a number of small aviaries. The aviary must consist of a shelter and an open and closed run (flight). If you construct the aviaries of wood, you'll need to use metal strips and wire mesh to protect it from gnawing, little beaks.

The aviary should be built in as dry a location as possible and one least affected by winds. The front of the aviary should face south (otherwise west). Plant hardy shrubs and small trees to provide sufficient shade.

Although a natural, earth floor has many advantages, I think that a cement or concrete floor is a better choice for breeding Cockatiels—and keeping them free of worms. On this floor, place large potted plants or pour the concrete so as to reserve several spots for planting shrubs. A cement floor can be hosed off daily, ridding it of any droppings and other messes the birds have made; or the floor could be sprinkled with sand or grit that should be replaced every two weeks. Part of the floor could be planted with sod; many Cockatiels very much enjoy frolicking on grass moist with dew or under the gentle spray of a garden hose. If you find it impossble to keep the sod alive, place it in low wooden boxes that can be removed whenever you wish to check or replace them without upsetting the birds.

It makes little difference where you place your aviary doors, as long as you remember to build two of them to form a little "foyer." This helps prevent your birds from escaping as you come into or leave the aviary. It is advisable to divide the flight from the shelter with a door as well; in this manner you encourage the birds to amuse themselves in the protected night shelter during particularly cold and nasty weather by simply closing the door.

Perches should be made of hardwood. Provide your Cockatiels with twigs and small branches from fruit trees and other safe trees and shrubs, so they can gnaw on these rather than the perches. Another advantage of providing twigs for gnawing is that the birds won't start the bad habit of pecking at each other's feathers. Affix the perches at both ends of the flight (run) so they do not interfere with the length of the flight available to the Cockatiels. Perches should not be installed too close to the wire, however, both because of cats, which are a definite danger, and because the Cockatiels' tail feathers would eventually become frayed when they are constantly rubbed against the wire. If you can place an old tree trunk in the center of the aviary or build the aviary around one, by all means use this arrangement.

Every aviary should be equipped with flat earthenware saucers allowing the birds to bathe. On colder days, of course, remove these dishes. Make sure your birds are dry before they go to sleep; they should not have the opportunity to bathe after four or five P.M. You could also put the garden sprinkler to good use, as many Cockatiels prefer this to a bath. Ponds with rocks and running water are obviously idyllic, but unfortunately not something that everyone can afford. Perches, of course, should not be situated above any of these bathing or drinking facilities. The water in the saucers should be changed daily.

Directions given in the chapter on feeding obviously pertain to both the pet owner who keeps one Cockatiel in a cage and the fancier who keeps several aviaries. However, one must realize that an aviary bird has a great deal more room for flying and hence gets much more exercise, so fat-containing seeds such as hemp, sunflower, linseed, maw, rape and peanuts can be given in greater quantities. Use indestructible seed feeders that are easily cleaned and made so the Cockatiels cannot soil their contents in any way and cannot sit or walk on seeds. Wooden feeders, of course, would soon be reduced to splinters. There are several feeders on the market. Your pet shop will be able to advise you on the best type for your circumstances. Saucers made of glass, ceramic, or similar materials are suitable as well and are most often used both for seed and for water.

The most practical feeders, however, are the box-like hoppers with glass fronts called self-feeders. These hoppers usually hold quantities of seeds sufficient for several days. They are often divided into a few narrow compartments in which each kind of seed is provided separately, enabling the birds to make their own mixture to suit an individual's needs. Around the bottom of these feeders extends a detachable tray that is designed to catch seeds thrown aside by the Cockatiels.

The Bird Room

The bird room is like an outside aviary as far as the furnishings are concerned, but it is usually located in an extra room in the house, sun room, an enclosed porch, the attic, etc. The "building" of the bird room is basically just installing wire screens in front of any windows and building a wire mesh "entrance hall" inside the door. The rest of the details are similar to the outside aviary. More valuable Cockatiel mutations are often kept in a bird room by experienced fanciers. However, this is not to say that beginning bird enthusiasts, working with less expensive birds, cannot attain excellent breeding results working with a bird room.

Obviously, such a bird-housing facility should be furnished to create as natural an effect as possible. The floor should consist of tiles upon which sand is sprinkled, which of course, must be replaced regularly. Try to maintain as much natural planting as possible, although the plants will need to be placed in pots and planters. With a little artistic insight you can create a beautiful piece of nature right in your own home!

The Room Aviary

The room aviary is also commonly used for keeping and even breeding Cockatiels; after all, heating is no problem here! This particular type of bird housing can best be described as follows: it is a small aviary that can be placed in any room or attic and in or around which are placed an abundance of plants; it houses one or three (never two) pairs of Cockatiels, depending on the size of the room aviary. The layout again is similar to that of the outside aviary.

Many people confuse a room aviary with a bird room. However, the bird room consists of an entire room not used by the residents of the house for anything but the birds, while a room aviary is an aviary located in a room. The room aviary has grown more popular in recent years, and there are even companies that build these aviaries ready-made and certainly satisfying the general requirements. I have seen some very lovely room aviaries in which successful breeding results were not uncommon, even though children played nearby daily.

The Cage

People are finding out more and more that Cockatiels are very easy birds to steady and finger tame; Cockatiels are, indeed, attractive to look at and although usually not very prolific talkers they will learn to repeat simple words and sentences. Cockatiels often become real household pets. In other words: they can be housed in a cage.

One of the main comments I can make on cages is that there is yet to be constructed a cage that is too big for our feathered friends. Even the well-known Budgerigar likes spaciousness. This is why I am not in favor of keeping Cockatiels in small cages; the bigger the better!

Cages should be constructed of metal, because those made of wood and such soon fall victim to the insatiable gnawing habits of our birds. If you can solder, you could probably build your own cage, but I think that in the long run you would spend less money buying a cage in a pet store. Almost every pet shop has a large selection of models, but the oblong shapes are my choice. A pair of Cockatiels (or one bird for that matter) can be happy in a cage that is 18 x 15 x 25 inches. The larger models are often equipped with a bottom that slides out, which simplifies cleaning and allows the bird to remain in the cage as well. Some have a double bottom, the top being made of wire bars like the rest of the cage. Personally I am not in favor of this variety, although it does mean that the birds do not step into their own feces. However, a compromise can be worked out here by covering part of the "grill" with a piece of grass sod, which of course will need to be replaced regularly. It is understandable that we should give an extra dish of grit to our Cockatiels if they are kept in a cage with a double bottom.

Even though you may be a "do-it-yourselfer," we still advise against a wooden cage. In spite of the fact that you may go to the trouble of covering the edges with metal strips, it will still just be a matter of time before the bird's gnawing damages the cage to the extent that it is no longer attractive and may end up in the garage, complete with the bird . . . hardly ideal air- and light-wise!

Perches are made of a hardwood such as beech and should not be too thin; 7/8 inch (22 mm) thick is ideal. Nor should they be too smooth; in fact, we should roughen them with sandpaper each time we clean the cage. Our Cockatiels have to get their rest on the perches, and they can't do this when the perches are too thin or too smooth. Their toes must comfortably clutch the perch in such a manner that the feet almost encircle the thickness of the perch, but not completely. The perches should be round but slightly flattened on the top to help prevent excessive growth of the nails. We advise using only hardwood perches because anything else would never last very long against the bird's gnawing. Softwood also has the disadvantage of being a good hiding place for insects, bacteria, and other undesirable inhabitants of your bird's cage. Perches that are too thin are also bad in that the toes will be hanging to the point where they are no longer protected by the feathers on the stomach when the bird is in a resting position. During the winter months this is very important, because if the feet are not adequately warmed by these feathers the bird will suffer from frozen toes. A good sitting or sleeping perch will allow the bird to rest comfortably and completely, and the stomach feathers will properly protect the feet.

To satisfy this need to gnaw and distract the birds from decimating the perches, give them twigs with which they can play and chew on to their hearts' content. Twigs from apple, pear, plum, cherry trees and fresh privet are ideal. These twigs (except the privet twigs) should be dried first (two weeks drying time is sufficient). In the aviary we can provide our birds with perches of various thicknesses, both stationary and swinging types, while the shrubbery we plant in the aviary will also provide ample resting places. Stationary perches should be placed in the inside area, thereby more or less forcing our birds to spend the night in the sheltered part. When your birds have developed the habit of sleeping in the night shelter, you will not be greeted with unpleasant surprises during the winter months. We can reinforce this habit even more by placing the stationary perches in high locations, particularly in the night shelter, because birds will instinctively go to the highest perches to sleep. Providing extra branches for climbing in the corners of the aviary is highly recommended because live shrubs and small trees are generally not guaranteed a very long life in an aviary with Cockatiels.

Back to the cage—the food and water dishes in a cage should be placed where no bird droppings can fall into them, as it would if they were placed underneath any perches. They should also be easily accessible to the bird keeper, since both food and water dishes should be cleaned daily. Naturally the seed dishes should be dried thoroughly before refilling. I recommend the

61

use of automatic feeding containers for seed and flat earthenware saucers for water. There should always be a cuttlebone available for the birds, as this provides some necessary minerals and is also excellent in helping to keep beaks in good shape.

Not all Cockatiels like to bathe, and certainly not when they are kept in cages. There are little metal "bath houses" that can be affixed to the opening of the cage, but many birds will never use them. They much prefer to frolic outside on a flat earthenware saucer, under a dripping faucet, or under a softly squirting garden hose. With tame birds this is easily arranged, but untamed Cockatiels will first have to become accustomed to their cage, their surroundings, and their keeper, before they can be offered a bath. In any event, be sure your birds are completely dry before they retire for the night. I can see no objection to placing bird and cage outside on a warm day and letting the garden hose softly drizzle on one side of it, to the greatest amusement of the bird(s). Obviously, the seed dish and the sand-covered bottom of the cage are removed so everything else can be thoroughly dried before bird and cage are taken back inside.

The location of the cage plays a significant role in the successful keeping of Cockatiels. Cockatiels (parakeets and parrots too for that matter) do not like to be alone, they like to belong to, and have the companionship of, the human family. They like to be in an area where they can observe all that goes on in the home. You should place the cage in a sunny location, although not directly in the sunlight, since the bird must have the opportunity to move to a shady spot if it wants to. In other words, part sun and part shade would be ideal. However, since the sun follows a set course, it may happen that at a certain time of the day the cage is completely within the rays of the sun. This is not good. Do not suppose that since Cockatiels come from Australia they will be used to sitting in and liking the sun. Although they come from the warm regions, the time they spend in direct sunlight is very limited, since they spend the largest part of their day in the shelter of the lush foliage of trees and such. In choosing the best location for the cage it is also very important that there is absolutely no draft. Therefore, avoid a location that is between doors and windows or in a corridor or hallway that has a door going outside. If the temperature generally remains the same both day and night, there is no need to cover the cage at night.

4

Diet and
Feeding Methods

DURING MY STAY IN AUSTRALIA I was able to observe Cockatiels at close range. While seed was ripening, they were sometimes seen on the ground in small groups looking for food. Not only grass seed is important—though this constitutes the chief ingredient on the menu—I have also seen birds eating all sorts of different weed, tree and shrub seeds. I also witnessed them feasting upon currant bushes whereas, much to the displeasure of the farmers, all kinds of fruit as well as various grains were eagerly consumed.

However, the so-called damage the birds are said to cause in this respect is strongly exaggerated and it is certainly not the Cockatiel the farmers and fruit growers should want to keep away from their fields. The birds are very fond of the seeds of the Acacia species, both those formed on the branches and those that have to be dug more or less from the ground with their proportionally, far from impressive bills. In this behavior (as in their menu) the Cockatiels strongly resemble the Cockatoos that also dig some of their food like turnips, carrots and seeds from the ground.

According to Forshaw, they also seem to eat the berries of the mistletoe (*Loranthus* sp.), although I have never witnessed this myself.

In this connection I must point out that cases are known of Cockatiels holding food with a foot, like Cockatoo species do. However, this behavior is rare.

In eastern Queensland I saw Cockatiels indulging in the sorghum crop. Especially after the breeding season when a great many young birds are added to the groups, quite some damage may be done, particularly when the birds are accompanied by the Red-rumped Parrot (*Psephotus haematonotus*)—and this occurs quite often.

I also frequently observed Cockatiels in blossoming eucalyptus trees (*Eucalyptus microtheca*), and here they appeared to enjoy the nectar from the flowers. It also seems to me that the insects visiting the flowers are not being ignored either. Many, if not all seed-eating birds consume more insects—especially during breeding time—than we would at first assume. I would not be astonished to discover that Cockatiels catch large quantities of small insects, spiders and snails daily. In captivity I have seen Cockatiels eating ant pupae! Thus, it is evident that Cockatiels in their natural state remain on the ground during the greater part of the day looking for grass and weed seed heads (especially *Astrebla* species). In this respect I will quote Dr. Greene once more. He says:

> The food of this species consists mainly of grass-seeds in their native wilds, and in captivity they seem to prefer canary-seed to any other, but when they have young ones to feed, they will eat, and seem to require, oats and bread-crumbs, soaked in cold water as well as dry, but not hard. The Cockatiel is undoubtedly a lazy bird, at least becomes so under domestication, and will never do for himself anything that he can get his owner to do for him. Thus, in the matter of feeding the young ones, there can be no doubt that in their native woods the parent birds forage far and near to provide their progeny with food, but in the bird-room or aviary, unless the food is just to their taste, and placed where they can readily reach it, they will rather let the young ones starve, than take the least trouble to fill their hungry little bellies, for they will not eat enough seed to feed both themselves and their young ones, but prefer to gobble up a quantity of bread, which does not need much preparation, and if a supply of this food fails, we have found that the young birds suffer [this is not always true!! M.M.V.]
>
> . . . It is almost superfluous to add here that the young of all the Parrot tribe do not gape, but are fed, as pigeons feed, by the old ones disgorging half-digested food from their own crops into the beaks of the babies, which they take into their own, both old and young making a pumping kind of motion, a bowing and scraping as one might say during the operation. And yet, such is the cimmerian darkness prevailing, even in high quarters, as to the domestic habits of birds, that, recently, we saw a picture, drawn by an eminent artist too, of a nestful of young Parrots, gaping as widely as a parcel of young thrushes might do, while they were being crammed by their parents with what looked like currant-buns, but was probably intended to represent some kind of fruit!
>
> . . . . Seed, we have said, constitutes the principal food of these birds, which are fond also of bread, and all kinds of green vegetables, from the flowering tufts of grass that grow by the wayside, to common lettuce and prosaic cabbage, the flowering tops of which last seem to afford them extreme delight. We may here mention, or rather repeat, that lettuce should never be given to captive birds until it has become "wilted," as the Americans say, in the sun, or even been kept a day or two in the house. Some Cockatiels we once kept in an aviary along with a pair

A Cockatiel in the wild. Note how well the bird's color blends with the background of a preferred nesting site.

Notwithstanding his Australian origin, the Cockatiel is a hardy bird and can even thrive as an aviary bird in northern climates, if properly conditioned. These normal-colored birds are not even fazed by the snow on the wires of their aviary. *Photo by author*

"I'll watch for them from this direction, you keep an eye on the other way." Pearled (left) and albino mutations. *Wissink*

The three grays and one dilute were all from the same brood. *Leysen*

An isabella dilute.

Wissink

A more recent mutation. Note the presence of white in the head and cheeks. *Wissink*

A normal-colored male in a typically alert posture. *Kwast*

"This is MY branch!" Gray Cockatiel photographed in its natural habitat.
Photo by author

Cockatiels kept in cages and aviaries are always more comfortable with natural perches. From his vantage point atop a small log, this pearled male surveys his domain. *Wissink*

Mutations have been developed and cultivated in many species. In the Cockatiel, the pearly mutation is highly prized for its unusually beautiful color and markings.

Even in mutant forms, secondary sexual characteristics often manifest themselves. Compare this demure, elegant pearled hen with the totally masculine cock on the previous page. *Photo by author*

of Red-crested Cardinals, were accustomed to partake so largely of the insect food, black beetles, mealworms, caterpillars, tipulae, etc., provided for the use of the latter, that we were compelled to remove them; which inclines us to the belief that in their wild state the Cockatiels, like many other members of the Parrot tribe, are by no means averse to an occasional tidbit in the shape of a fat grub, a white ant or two, or any other succulent insect morsel they may chance to fall in with; but in captivity they do perfectly well without such exceptional dainties; we are, however, without any data as to their habits in this respect in their native wilds, and the insect-eating proclivities of our Cockatiels may quite as well have been an instance of depraved appetite, as a reversion to an ancestral and natural habit.

Green indeed was close to the "real manners" of the Cockatiels in the wild, but don't forget, that this doctor of medicine was writing in 1884. And I still think—as an ornithologist and aviculturist—that Greene's book, *Parrots in Captivity*, *is* one of the greatest books on the subject. Understandably, much of Greene's text is now outdated, although I feel that the descriptions of the different parrots, as well as the beautiful pictures, cannot be improved upon.

Back to reality.

Feeding Domestic Birds

When Cockatiels are kept in a cage or aviary, a rich variety of food should be available. Like people, Cockatiels are individualists (although in their natural state they are usually seen in groups) and what one bird likes the other may ignore. But we have seen just now that Cockatiels feed mainly on all sorts of seeds from the ground or from low shrubs and trees. These seeds may be ripe or half ripe. Australia is known for its large grass varieties.

In captivity, Cockatiels, among other species, normally receive a mixture of hard, often very dry seeds. The two most important kinds are millet or canary seed. However, millet does not contain enough lysin and arginine. Lysin is absolutely necessary both for young and adult birds, as it is found in their feather pigment. A lack of it results in a poor pigmentation of the feathers. Arginine is also an amino acid and extremely important for the feather albumin, so that it is an absolute "must" all during the bird's life. Both amino acids belong to the 10 so-called essential amino acids (the other eight being: histidine, isoleucine, leucine, methionine, fenylalanine, threonine, tryptophane and valine). A temporary lack of one of these acids impedes the adequate formation of albumin, whereas a chronic shortage irrevocably results in the bird's death, because the worn-out body tissues are no longer replaced by others.

In the open country, Cockatiels (and other birds of course) will at once make up for such a shortage, for instance by eating insects (so Greene observed correctly). It has been proven that the greater part of these insects contain a rather considerable amount of lysin. Arginine is found in any albumin. Besides, it will be clear to anybody that ripe seeds will contain substantially fewer vitamins than those that are half-ripe.

In connection with this, shortages of essential amino acids may result in the so-called "runners" or "crawlers" (French molt) with Budgerigars. This means that when they have left the nestbox, nestlings are unable to fly as their feathers are undeveloped. So it is absolutely essential that the birds are properly fed. As we are entirely dependent on the pet store to supply food material, the food offered will have to be rich and varied.

What to Feed

Before commenting on nutrients other than seed, I will first list a daily menu to be offered to the birds. Naturally, this does not suffice, but the main daily requirements are met:

1/4 oz. of mixed seeds, namely white or canary seed, millet, Italian millet, hulled oats and small sunflower seeds;

3/4 oz. of green food, namely (by choice): chickweed with its tiny white flowers (grows in most gardens), lettuce, endive, dandelions, shepherd's purse, spinach, chickory, soaked and germinated grass and weed seeds, branches (those of willows and fruit trees, and especially privet; the leaves certainly are a favorite green food for Cockatiels);

quarter of a sweet apple and occasionally a piece of banana (once a week);

1/2 oz. of whole-meal bread, half of which is soaked in milk;

1/4 oz. of minerals, namely cuttlebone, mineralized pieces of calcium, grit, etc.; there is a large variety available on the market.

Note: during the breeding season: about 1/5 oz. of plain cake, mixed with honey and soaked in milk in addition to rearing foods (use a reliable brand) for large parakeets and for Budgerigars.

It goes without saying that these are the *minimum requirements* regarding nourishment. Throughout the year, certain needs will increase, as is the case with other animals; also Cockatiels in captivity require the richest possible varied menu.

Remember that a high quality diet is vitally important to the degree of success for the bird lover's efforts. So this means that the food composition for Cockatiels must contain every conceivable nutrient necessary for their growth and energy supply.

This also implies that the required vitamins, minerals and trace elements must be included as well.

The albumin needed for any bird's growth should therefore guarantee a proper pattern of amino acids. When certain materials are lcaking in the

74

albumin, the process of growth may stagnate. Also during molting, the feather formation will not progress smoothly when the daily food ration contains too few essential amino acids.

Farina (= starch), sugar, fat and oils serve for the energy supply, and not for growth! So from these energy sources, the birds cannot produce any feathers during molting time, but only use them for energy purposes in order to bring their body temperature up to the norm.

Energy foods are crucial, for they enable all the other vital functions, like walking, flying, pairing and breeding to be performed.

The amount of energy foods the birds have to ingest again depends on their housing conditions. In warm surroundings, an overdose of farina, sugars, fat and oils in the daily ration will very soon give rise to an excessive formation of fat in the bird's body. So seeds that are rich in oils, such as sunflower, hemp, and niger must only be given in moderate quantities.

The following food composition which fully provides for the Cockatiels' needs during the various phases of life, has proven very successful to many aviculturists:

Seed Mixture During the Breeding Season and Molting Period

47% white millet and/or La Plata millet
18% white or canary seed
15% sunflower seed
8% hulled oats
5% hemp
4% niger seed   Calculated protein (raw) = 13.4%
3% buckwheat   Calculated fat (raw) = 13.7%

Total: 100%

Seed Mixture During the "Resting" Period

62% white millet and/or La Plata millet
15% white or canary seed
12% sunflower seed
4% hulled oats
2% hemp
2% niger seed   Calculated protein (raw) = 12.6%
3% buckwheat   Calculated fat (raw) = 8.6%

Total: 100%

In the above mixtures we clearly see the difference between the figures in food value. For times that our birds have to produce, these figures are adapted. The difference of 5.1% of raw fat is especially striking. We have arrived at these mixtures in order to prevent the formation of a surplus of fat in the birds through which they could become unsuitable for breeding.

It is understandable that the aviculturist should offer these mixtures in a sensible manner; in other words by offering our birds enough seeds they will decide for themselves which seed to take; the rest of the offered seeds will be neglected and often scattered around, and thus lost.

It is also clear to everyone that additional foods must be supplied as well during the breeding period and during the time the parents are raising their young.

Apart from the above I personally feel it necessary to point out that each pair of Cockatiels must have *free access* to the following seeds, even when you offer the above named mixtures: panicum millet, canary seed, white millet and La Plata millet, buckwheat and some hemp and hulled oats, niger seed, spray millet and—in case the birds have somewhat thin and watery droppings—poppy seed. I believe that it is wise if we let our birds be their own doctors in captivity. Therefore they must have free access to the best possible seeds, and the ones mentioned are—for Cockatiels—indeed the best. If you prefer to give those seeds as a mixture, this is your choice, although it is wise to especially keep the given percentages between the two mixtures in mind.

During the breeding period germinated seeds, grass and wheat seeds are absolutely essential. Twice a week a few peanuts are also welcome. Don't give more as they are very fattening. For this reason I am against offering Cockatiels peanuts when they are housed in a cage or small indoor flight.

During the breeding season—next to germinated seeds and seeds in husks—cooked corn is a necessity as well. During molting time and in the spring it won't do any harm if the birds can freely make use of it.

Many fanciers like to offer the various seeds in a single food-cup or in seed-containers with separated compartments rather than offering a mixture of seeds. This is based simply on the fact that each bird should be its own physician. A Cockatiel, if he is permitted to choose from a mixture of seeds, chooses those he needs at that particular time.

My birds have the opportunity to eat millet spray all year round and they all love it! One of the first seeds young Cockatiels will eat, as soon as they are no longer being fed by their parents, is indeed millet spray. It can also be used as a treat during training. During the breeding season each pair will receive, regardless of whether they have eggs or are nourishing young, millet spray that has been soaked for 24 hours, and dried with a towel; the birds are crazy about it. Be sure to remove all the soaked millet that has not been eaten by evening, to prevent mould and/or deterioration.

If the aviculturist is away from home for long periods, it sometimes becomes impossible to perform all the required tasks and necessary food preparations. In these circumstances, commercial seed mix will suffice now and again. By checking the contents on the wrapper it will be easy to see how closely it conforms to our own, set food requirements. Avoid mixtures containing too much sunflower seed and hemp, seeds that are appreciated very much by all Cockatiels, but can only be offered in small quantities due to their high fat contents (as is proven clearly by the two mixtures above). This is especially true for birds kept in cages, as their opportunity for great activity is extremely limited in comparison to the "fun and games" of those birds housed in large, outdoor aviaries. The latter will lose fat much more quickly, as you will undoubtedly understand.

During the breeding period it is essential as well that the birds have all kinds of greens and fruit available. Personally I think it absolutely necessary that these be fed in generous quantity the whole year round. Excellent greens are: chickweed, chopped dandelion (also the whole plant, roots and all), lettuce, endive, spinach, carrot-tops and—of course you guessed it—the leaves of the privet, as the birds never seem to get enough of this.

A few branches daily also means a real feast for the birds.

I regard germinated seeds as green food. Much is eaten during the breeding season. The same applies for cooked corn, as it is excellent as rearing-food. Further, willow branches and branches of practically all fruit trees are indispensable. Watch out, however, that none of the offered branches, fruits or greens are ever sprayed with insecticides, as this can be extremely dangerous, indeed quite often fatal for all your birds.

Each day offer fresh branches. By putting them in a glass jar with water, they remain fresher much longer; the jar itself can be buried into the ground, up to its rim, and provided with a mesh "lid," in which you place the branches.

Beside the rich food value the offering of fresh branches represents, there is a great therapeutic value as well; the birds will work at them and so will not get bored, which in turn means that they will have no time either to pick each others' feathers or become cannibalistic—two common behavior problems that often occur if the birds don't have anything to do.

Don't make the mistake, as so many aviculturists apparently do, of thinking that lettuce alone does the trick; in other words that it will provide enough vitamins, etc. This is not true, as lettuce contains about 95% water.

The safest way to offer greens are greens from your own yard. Only then can you be certain that these greens are not sprayed with insecticides. Washing and shaking them dry are by no means a safeguard. That greens bought at a supermarket are harmless to the birds is not true either. And do you know that the already mentioned dandelion is richer in vitamins than many so-called cultivated vegetables; the same can be said for chickweed.

Throughout the year, but especially during the breeding period, one can supply an excellent rearing food with crumbled old bread (as Dr. Greene stated earlier), mixed with small mealworms, ant pupae, other live food and hard-boiled egg. The commercially available rearing mixes for parakeets and Budgerigars are also excellent, as much research is put into them.

When feeding mealworms, it is advisable to kill them by putting them in an old nylon stocking and dipping them in boiling water for 30 seconds, as full-grown worms are able to penetrate a Cockatiel's stomach wall. (Birds swallow all food whole, they don't chew.)

It is best to experiment with commercial foods: mark the cups in which you offer the brands and see how the birds react. Birds are individuals like any other living creature and will quickly show preferences for certain foods. Of course, only the chosen brand(s) should be offered to your Cockatiels.

During the breeding season I like to offer my birds plain cake and/or brown bread, soaked in milk. They relish this, and so do their young. The parents will gladly give it to the youngsters in the nest. And that is just what we want, as cow's milk contains lysin, so very important for good featter growth (a deficiency of lysin is often manifested by yellow feathers scattered throughout the body plumage).

Vitamins and Minerals

With the rearing food I always mix some vitamin AD, B^2 and B^{12} drops, according to the information on the instructions. I also add a few drops daily to the drinking water as a substantial portion of the strength of vitamins is lost in ripe, dry seeds. Seeds are also low in minerals and natural salts, and these are in turn indispensable for animal tissue. Therefore, one must include minerals as well "on the bird menu." Calcium, for instance, is necessary for the formation of bone and strong egg shells. Therefore cuttlebone, grit and pieces of mortar should be available to your birds throughout the year.

Grit or gravel has the double purpose of grinding up the food and furnishing indispensable minerals not always present in other feed. Messrs Bates and Busenbark advise using crushed granite, as sand is worn smooth and is therefore not a satisfactory grinding agent. Through the grinding process the digestive juices can work into the food better and so the birds will get more nutrition from it. Grit and such can best be given in flat earthen dishes and are best not mixed with other minerals. Cuttlebone, mortar and mineral blocks should be fixed securely in the cage or aviary so the birds have easy access to them.

Don't supply cuttlebone as the only calcium source. The salt content in cuttlebone is often too high, and as a result too much fluid is retained in the body cells. Cuttlebone found on the beach must first be soaked in fresh water (change the water at least three times a day for four days), as seaside, fresh cuttlebone is much too salty for the birds.

In spite of a rich seed variety, Cockatiels—like many other cage and aviary birds, known as so-called seed eaters—eat small quantities of their own and other droppings. This is mostly done to counter vitamin deficiencies. There are many important vitamins in droppings, such as practically all the B-vitamins, but especially B^2 (riboflavin) and B^{12} (cyanocobalamine). So don't be alarmed when you see this occurring in your aviary or cage, as this phenomenon is quite common in the wild with birds and mammals as well (think of wolves, dogs, rabbits, horses etc.); where droppings, as said, of "colleagues" are sometimes eaten.

They Must Have Water

Due to the nature of their diet and a large proportion of green food, Cockatiels do not drink often. But, like all living things, birds must have fresh, clean water daily; this can be tap or rainwater. If your tap water is too high in calcium content, rainwater could be preferable, although highly-calcified water is not harmful when it is offered just before the breeding season.

Many aviculturists think it necessary to boil the drinking water. But boiled water is far from tasty, it is "flat," and therefore uninviting to the birds.

Drinking water can be offered in the same type of dishes used for seed, or you may want to consider using drinking fountains. As long as the birds will use them, and as long as they are safe in design, there is no objection to these.

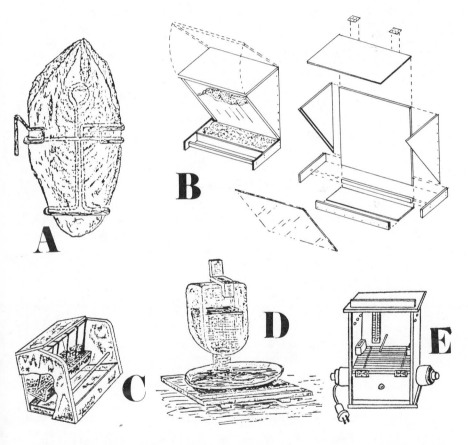

A. Cuttlebone in a holder. An essential source of minerals, cuttlebone contains a very high percentage of calcium carbonate though samples may vary considerably. B. Components and assembly of a useful bird feeder. C. A different type of feeder. D. An old bottle makes a good fountain. E. A hospital cage. *Drawings by the author*

Fountains keep water fresher and cleaner longer than possible in open dishes, in which all kinds of dirt and bacteria can thrive. Nevertheless I do prefer open dishes for cages and aviaries, provided they are cleaned daily, and filled with fresh water at least twice a day (in the morning and late afternoon). Never situate these dishes near or under perches and other roosting places, and far enough away from seed and grit cups. Cockatiels like to bathe exexuberantly more than once a day and will splash everything around them, including food!

Treats—Good and Bad

In conclusion I would like to draw your attention to the following: many fanciers think it necessary (they are even positive that they are doing their pets a great favor) to let Cockatiels eat with them during meals. These birds receive beer-soaked pieces of bread, pieces of old cheese, pastry, butter-biscuits, bacon rinds or a slice of sausage. Sooner or later these birds will be damaged irrevocably. *Never* offer fat-containing food or alcohol to any bird. A piece of fresh cheese, now and again, one cube (½ sq. inch) of raw, red beef daily (if they will accept it; not every Cockatiel likes beef though); a crust of brown bread are all acceptable tidbits within bounds. Offering all kinds of goodies may, perhaps, speak of your love and attachment for your bird, but in reality you're not doing the animal any favors; far from it! Offer only proper feed and pay constant attention to the quality of the feed that is given.

Feeding Routine

Make it a point to feed your birds at the same time each day, preferably in the morning before work.

Fill all water and seed cups and don't be afraid that the birds will overeat, a thought still vividly alive among fanciers. Cups can be cleared of husks by blowing over the seeds. Make a habit of filling the cups with fresh seeds every other day, which means that all the seeds are spread out over a newspaper and thoroughly cleaned of all husks. The remaining seeds can be put back into the cup, and replenished with new seed.

Spoiled and old feed must be removed immediately. Note, that during warm, especially humid days, certain feed can spoil quickly, such as egg-food and greens. So keep an eye on those.

5

Breeding Cockatiels

BIRDLOVERS who take their hobby seriously will sooner or later want to start breeding. Breeding Cockatiels is relatively easy partly because they have been domesticated for so long. By starting with good, healthy birds, which are not related, your results will not be without merit.

Foundation Stock

A breeding season stands and falls with the *quality* of the foundation stock but most of all with the female. She must be absolutely healthy and full of life. She should on no account have any disorder of her digestive system or anything similar. She should not lay eggs that are too small, brood restlessly, feed the young birds badly or pluck their feathers.

Birds brought up by a "bad" hen (assuming she could create a family at all) are unfit for further breeding. Don't seek out trouble at the beginning, so be scrupulously selective and do not breed from such females.

The male too should be in good condition of course. He should not pluck the feathers of the chicks either. A good male wants to assist his female with the breeding and rearing of his young; he should show interest in what happens in the nestbox and in the breeding-place. He must not try to copulate before the earlier brood has flown out. As you see, the right male is also subject to strict selection, if you want to breed birds of good quality.

Breeding success is guaranteed once you have a good breeding pair. Be very careful with such birds and never breed them more than three times per season. Even good pairs will, if given the chance, go on breeding until winter. In preparation for the breeding season, start providing calcium, minerals, trace elements and vitamins (there are several different preparations on the market, which can be mixed in with the seed). I give all my birds this necessary food all year, as well as grit, cuttlebone, seaweed and phosphate mixtures.

Three times a week I mix some glucose into the drinking water. I feel this is an indispensable product which has a positive effect on the total physical condition. It is especially ideal for Cockatiels that have a large flight at their disposal. Regularly provided it gives the liver a reserve. Glucose is also ideal for newly-purchased birds.

The Breeding Season

The period in which you begin breeding your birds is also very important. The danger of an early start is that early spring weather is generally unpredictable. It may lead to failures if the cold holds on and if there are still some frosty nights. It doesn't make very much difference if the nest boxes are hanging in the night shelter of the aviary; the early morning temperatures will often be too low. When the birds leave their nests to relieve themselves and to feed and drink, if the changeover with the mate is not immediately effected, the results to eggs or infant birds can be disastrous.

Personally I start the breeding season in late March or early April—some of the birds may turn out to be late breeders. This method, however is only used—together with winter breeding—if you want to have fully grown, good birds for early shows. Cockatiels need at least eight months to a year, sometimes even longer (depending primarily on the mutation) to be ready for showing. New show birds should be fully grown, done with molting. Birds which are not yet fully grown and are still molting, usually lay small eggs, stop laying eggs or stop breeding, could start molting suddenly or suffer from egg binding.

We keep a breeding record to know the descent (and other information) of our Cockatiels.

If you start early anyway, say in winter, in spite of the explanation above, some way of lighting the aviary will be absolutely necessary, for the nights are too long to make the birds breeding-ready. Therefore you need a timer. The lighting must be lengthened gradually to fourteen or fifteen light hours. Use fluorescent lights as these give twice as much light as ordinary bulbs and the energy cost is considerably lower.

Breeding Behavior

We know, from experience, that sometimes Cockatiels start breeding more easily in a large cage or small aviary rather than in a large, outside aviary. This applies mostly to birds that are very shy and which react with panic at the least disturbance; thereby flying into the wire netting or aviary wall, while screeching loudly, with sad results of course. However you will

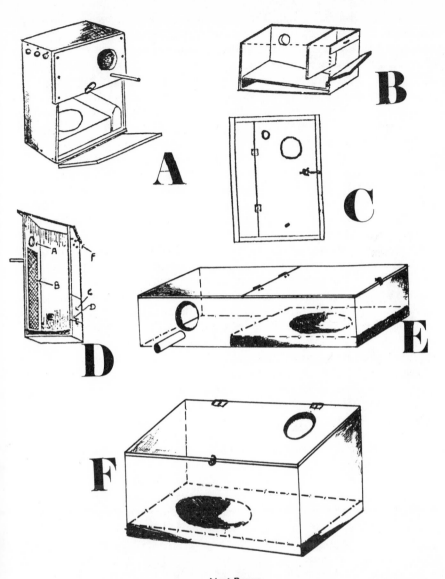

Nest Boxes

A. Wooden nest box opened to show the removable, concave base. B. The sliding bottom of this nest box will discourage hens with the unfortunate tendency to eat their own eggs, by keeping the eggs out of reach. C. Every nest box should be equipped with a side entrance hole. D. Another type of useful nest box equipped as follows:
A) Entrance B) Wire netting to help birds climb in and out C) Inspection Door D) Lock E) Concave base F) Additional Ventilation Holes
E. A roomy nest box birds like. F. If the bird breeder uses this model nest box, he must provide wire netting for the back wall as with diagram D.

Designs and drawings by the author

of somewhat rougher wood. They don't like boxes made of hardboard or other materials, although these boxes are available in pet stores. I prefer a long nest box; the advantage of this type is that the opening for the Cockatiel to enter the box can be made in the right or left side corner, away from the nest-hollow, which prevents the bird from landing on the eggs. Many eggs are lost this way, as they get damaged and thus become useless. Large staples or a strip of wire mesh on the inside of the box makes it easier for the bird to climb in and out. Watch for burrs on the wire netting as the birds can easily injure themselves on these. It is also recommended that you make the bottom of the box removable, so that the inside of the box can be cleaned thoroughly after a breeding season. A small door or detachable roof is also handy to make checking feasible. It is possible that birds won't accept nest boxes which are made of smooth planks (spruce fir, birch, beech, oak, willow). If we place pieces of bark against the sides (you will be able to get those at garden centers or pet stores), the willingness to accept these boxes will be greater. Boxes made out of hardwood of course last longer than those made out of other kinds of wood. Cockatiels have a notorious love of gnawing, so watch out. See to it that the bottom of the box has a thickness of at least 1½ inches to lessen the loss of breeding heat. Nest boxes with a double bottom are very useful, as you can place a small bowl of water between the two floors. In the upper floor on which the eggs lay, drill a few holes to guarantee the right humidity which is needed to help the eggs hatch. You will also notice more than once that a breeding bird takes a water bath before he or she sits on the eggs, with wet feathers. Their "wild" ancestors left them this "working method." Because the Cockatiel is strongly domesticated, it often happens that pairs never bathe before taking their place on the eggs; that's why a nest box with a double bottom is so useful.

Always give your Cockatiels a choice; therefore hang nest boxes of different wood types and models, and place them in assorted (but always high) locations. We put some rotted wood (my preference goes to willow) mixed with sawdust and black earth (which should under no circumstance hold any fertilizer!) in the nest hollow; also peat or moist moss are very useful. Don't give too much—a layer of about ¼ inch—otherwise the birds will only throw out any surplus, which sometimes takes them days to do. It also wastes valuable time during the breeding season. I also have much success with boxes, that do not have a double bottom, but instead have a moist layer of grass/sod and on top of that some peat, sawdust and rotted willow wood.

Egg Laying, Brooding and Hatching

A Cockatiel hen lays four to seven white eggs (about 1 inch x ¾ inch), sometimes more. Keep the clutch at five to six eggs, because more eggs are difficult to cope with for one pair. It's often wise to distribute the eggs of larger

86

clutches among other pairs, assuming of course they all started breeding at about the same time. Rosemary Low commented on this as follows:

The average clutch size is five. When the Parrot Society took census among breeders of Cockatiels in 1969, the statistics of members who replied produced the following interesting figures: 41 pairs laid 430 eggs in 86 clutches (average of five per clutch). The largest clutch was seven (in six cases) and the smallest two and three (seven cases). Of the eggs laid, 58 percent produced chicks—a percentage which would surely prove higher than that for most other species of parrots, were similar censuses held. In only three of the 86 clutches were all the young reared. The nest box size most commonly used was 25 cm (10 inch) square and 46 cm (18 inch) high. The highest number of young raised in one year was 14 (three clutches of five, four and five); the second largest was 11. The oldest parent was a 19-year-old male (*Magazine of the Parrot Society,* February, 1970). Miss N. Taylor reported (1978) that her pair had reared 68 young in five years; perhaps not a record but a most creditable total.

When I read articles like this I often think that some breeders degrade their birds to "laying hens." The females weaken and suffer egg binding. I cannot caution you enough about egg binding; if you do not notice it in time it might mean the death of the hen. As I have already pointed out, do not start with females that are too young; give them enough food which contains sufficient vitamins, minerals and greens. Watch for females that have a tendency to develop egg binding (often through heredity or physical deviation) especially those that lay overlarge eggs.

See to it also that the birds that are wormed by a veterinarian are not kept together with fowl, and are not exposed to extreme temperature differences. Also watch out that in-breeding is not pushed too far, and that the breeding area (if the breeding is to take place indoors) is not too dry. There is no harm in candling the eggs quickly, once the clutch is complete, so we can determine the position of the embryo; the best time to do this is one week after the bird has started brooding. It is possible that the chick is positioned incorrectly; the head should be close to the airchamber; it will be very hard for the young bird to free itself if this is not the case. Sometimes it will not be able to free itself at all. Also watch that the breeding pairs are not overconditioned or too fat, which happens often with beginners as they are inclined to be over-anxious.

Some good advice: join a local bird-club and talk to experienced breeders to obtain advice; even if you hear many different opinions you'll always pick up something useful.

Nest observation is indicated only when absolutely necessary. You will know when the eggs are hatching by the sounds you hear. It is no problem at all if some eggs hatch a day or so later than others, as long as you register them properly in your breeding record. Never break any eggs open to help the hatching chick; help is only needed when it is clear that a chick sticks to the eggshell with its head or wings! Remember that when a nest is inspected too often the parents may abandon the chicks.

The brooding is performed by both parents; the male broods from

A seven-day-old chick covered with a sparse coat of yellow down. This chick has just been fed, resulting in a bulging crop. Cockatiel young have very large crops so need handfeeding about five times a day. Later, according to Bates and Busenbark "when they are beginning to feather, they need to be foraged only three times a day, but the chicks might benefit if the meals came slightly more frequently than this. Apart from food, the very young chicks need to be kept warm until they are three weeks old. If too cold, they will not feed with any enthusiasm nor can they digest their food efficiently; they could pine away and die, or, at best, grow slowly. For the first week the chicks might be kept at about 95°-100° F. (35°-38° C.), dropping to 80° F. (27° C.) at two weeks. When too warm the chicks will pant and take on a rich pink color and the temperature should be dropped by 5° F. (3° C.)." *Photo by author*

morning until late afternoon, the female takes over the task for the remaining time. It is unusual to see both parents on the nest at the same time.

I should point out that it does happen that the male just will not take part in the process of brooding; this is often the case with young inexperienced males. There is not much you can do about it and that is why it is better to start with partners that are at least two years old. Of course there are different opinions about this. If the male persists in his attitude it is best to give the female another mate; the first male should not be used for further breeding purposes. You may give it another try however, perhaps the following season, but chances that it will go well are minimal. It is wise however, when a young, inexperienced pair do not give good breeding results, to give both birds other mates.

Remember, the best results are obtained if the birds are able to choose their own partners. To accomplish this, bring together in a large aviary different young birds that have not yet mated. Provide an even number of males and females and put colored rings around their legs. After a couple of days you will notice which birds are interested in each other.

Back to the eggs. There are still aviculturists who will try to clean dirty eggs (especially eggs with droppings on them) with a piece of absorbent cotton and lukewarm water. Do not do this! It will only clog up more egg-pores, and make it harder for oxygen to get in, and so brings us from bad to worse. Leave dirty eggs alone; nine out of ten times they'll hatch anyway. Cracked eggs have to be removed of course. A very tiny crack can sometimes be successfully repaired with a piece of tape or some nail polish. Generally this does not help and any cracked eggs should be considered lost.

The young Cockatiels will hatch after a period of about 19-21 days, depending on the temperature outside. They will be covered with soft, yellow down. It is essential that there be absolute rest for the first couple of hours after hatching. This is important as the birds are easily startled. It is even possible that the parents will give up brooding completely. If they do not (with luck) the brooding time will be longer. Nest observation is still necessary of course, but must be done with care. This also applies as the chicks grow; there is nothing wrong with a look into the box every so often; the chicks will even try to impress you by swaying their small bodies and hissing like kittens.

Watch from a distance (I use binoculars) and check to see if the young are being fed properly. If this is not the case the young will have to be hand-fed or you will have to find them foster-parents.

Caring for Young Birds

Many aviculturists wish to band their birds; I use rings with a diameter of 1/5 inch. Do not band your birds too early. There is no set time for this, because it depends on the speed with which the chicks grow; young that are fed well grow faster than those that are not.

A baby albino Cockatiel at 12 days old, being hand-fed. *Mathews*

The same baby at 15 days. *Mathews*

At 20 days the baby Cockatiel has grown considerably.

At five weeks the young Cockatiel is almost fully feathered. It is interesting to note that even though this bird is albino, it does have color in its crest, cheek patches and under the tail. *Mathews*

The birds are usually banded between the seventh and tenth day. Blacken the ring by holding it over a burning candle as shiny rings will sometimes lead to anxiety; the parent birds will often want to remove them from the nest and whether there is a young bird attached to this shining "thing" does not really make any difference.

The band is first pushed over the two front toes that have been "glued" together with vaseline; the two back toes are "glued" to the leg, after which the ring is pushed further. The banding of Cockatiels should take place in the evening, as the parents' urge to keep the nest clean has then lessened somewhat.

Some people think that young birds become sick easily and because of this wash their hands before handling them. It may sound a little strange however but do not wash your hands at all. Rub them thoroughly with a grass sod, so that our human odor will be dispelled.

Next to greens as rearing food and old bread soaked in water (avoid milk as it turns sour quickly) mixed with a mashed, hardboiled egg-yolk, you may provide sprouted grass and weed seeds, as well as soaked and sprouted millet sprays. Cockatiels enjoy grass seeds still in the sheath, fruit and sometimes mealworms.

The chicks leave the nest when they are four to five weeks old, but will still receive food from the parents for at least another three to four weeks. It is wise to remove the young birds from cage or aviary if the parents start a new breeding round. They will start to feed on their own anyway and show other signs of independence. Provide these young Cockatiels with a special, small aviary (baby-pen or -flight). For the time being give them the same food they were accustomed to when they were still being fed by their parents. Also supply seeds in abundance, the usual Cockatiel menu, plus water in a shallow bowl. Never give water in a bowl with a rim turned upwards as the possibility exists that when the birds lift their heads after drinking, they will get stuck behind this rim and drown.

Young Cockatiels from the last breeding round can be left with the parents until autumn (the nest boxes have been taken away of course). Young from the first two breeding rounds have now become totally independent. They have flown around in the baby-flight for about three to four weeks, and can be put in their own aviary where they will have enough room to fly around, climb, and develop into healthy adults. Every so often one or more of the young birds will sit with fluffed feathers and look ill, also the area around the vent may be swollen and inflamed. Place these birds apart and feed them old white or brown bread that has been soaked in milk (change the mixture every two hours; if the weather is hot do not make more than the birds can eat in 15 minutes), and add a pinch of bicarbonate of soda to it. Do this for about three days. The condition is usually the result of having eaten seeds in the hull too rapidly. So let the birds continue the first couple of weeks on their rearing-food.

Because it broke in the nest box, this egg became "glued" to the chest of the cock shown here. This is a rare kind of accident in an aviary or Nature. It took several days for the bird to lose his egg! *Oberink*

Handfeeding young birds often results in wonderfully tame pets that are particularly devoted to people. *Courtesy Ruth Hanessian*

After three months the beak will change from flesh color to a darker shade, and the birds will start to molt, which, if everything goes well, ends at about nine months. Biologically speaking these Cockatiels are sexually mature at that time, but the aviculturist is better to wait at least another eight months before setting them up for breeding. Remember, the best nests come from pairs that are about two years old.

Often the female will start a second round before her first young are completely independent. It even happens that she starts a second round with the young of the first brood still in the nest. Be careful in such situations, as often the male will chase his offspring. So take the young from the aviary at once and feed them by hand until they are full-grown. If you have an opportunity to clean the nest box before the second round (and third), then do so, to prevent lice and other parasites.

Finally, it is very difficult—and this also applies for the different color mutations—to determine the sex of immature Cockatiels, and this will only be possible after long observation. You can distinguish the sexes since the birds that sing are males. You can also inspect the outer edge of the outer tail-feathers if you do not have the time for long observations. These are feathers of an even yellow or greyish yellow color if the bird is a *female,* while the tailfeathers of the *male* are always speckled. However, when the birds are albino, or pied with white tail-feathers, this method cannot be applied.

Artificial Breeding and Handfeeding

Unfortunately, it often happens that after the female has laid her eggs, she will not return to the nest and the clutch to brood. When the female doesn't have sufficient brood urge, there may be many reasons; housing and feeding seem to bear heavily upon this behavior. When housing and feeding are as they should be, however, we will not often experience a situation where the female doesn't start brooding. Unfortunately, the female may also ignore her eggs in good aviaries and when she receives excellent care.

In most cases the female will start to brood after the second egg. So if you notice that the bird doesn't make any preparations at all to incubate her eggs after the second, or sometimes third egg, you must intervene, at least if you want to prevent the loss of the eggs. When the hatch is complete and the female is not interested in brooding, remove the eggs carefully and lay them in a cool place, where they can certainly keep for about 10 to 12 days, probably even longer.

As I advise you to build an electric incubator (using an assembly kit) or buy one, the storage of the eggs for some time is useless. I can imagine, though, that a breeder of various species and with one "artificial mother" would like to know whether it is possible to keep eggs over a certain period. That is certainly possible!

I place the eggs of a non-brooding female in my incubator when another possibly related female starts brooding. After six days all the eggs in the incubator, and those of the intended foster-parent, are inspected; all unfertilized eggs are destroyed and the good eggs from the incubator are placed in the nest of the brooding female. Don't place these eggs in the nest arbitrarily; it's better to wait, until the brooding female leaves the nest to limber up a little, or when she is being fed by the male near the delivery room. Many experienced breeders have special breeding pairs that only act as foster-parents and have never before raised a hatch of their own.

Indeed, this is especially so with Cockatiels; yet, you should be aware that the chances of success are only so/so, but as a breeder, you run that risk, like it or not.

After having considered suitable foster-parents you now come to the actual brooding. My greatest success and the best final results is with the previously mentioned small-model electric incubator, in which the egg-drawer lies horizontally and is made of small-mesh wire-netting. On this lies a piece of coarse jute to prevent the young birds from stepping through the wire-netting of the egg-drawer and possibly fracturing a leg.

The incubator is heated by hot air which flows from above over the eggs and is drained off along one of the side-walls or from below through the ventilation holes. I achieve the best results with a constant temperature of 105° F (39.5°C); this is the temperature just above that of the eggs. A thermostat regulates the temperature. A thermometer is needed, of course, and is usually built into the incubator—otherwise it would be impossible to ascertain whether the temperature still meets our requirements.

Install the thermometer just above the eggs, against one of the side-walls so that the mercury-bulb is at the height of the eggs. The incubator itself has double walls, naturally, to guarantee good insulation; in this way an equable distribution of warmth is achieved.

I recommend the *ether-capsule*-thermostat, as it is the most sensitive, and therefore, accurate unit. It is better than the bi-metallic-thermostat, which is widely used because of its solidity, but which is not as sensitive as the ether-capsule type.

I daresay we have all heard at one time or another, that birds turn over their eggs many times a day for reasons we can understand. With no birds to do the job in the incubator, you must turn the eggs yourself—twice a day. Don't be afraid the eggs will cool off too fast by your opening the incubator door; this "airing" is even necessary to ensure a good growth in the eggs, because it provides fresh oxygen.

It is best to turn the eggs near eight o'clock in the morning and again about nine in the evening. Be careful when you turn the eggs not to break the shell; use a plastic spoon rather than your fingers. When you turn the eggs in the morning, check that there is still sufficient water in the drawer at the bottom of the incubator to ensure proper humidity. Only then can you be sure that the eggs won't dry out and that the young will hatch from them properly.

94

Many people use a so-called *hygrometer* to measure the humidity, but I believe this is not exactly necessary for the smaller machines: usually such meters are already supplied with the machine.

When the young are at the point of emerging, the eggs can be placed under a brooding bird; her own clutch is taken away and usually has to be considered lost, but it can also be placed in the incubator, so that you create a closing circle as it were.

With more brooding pairs, we can distribute the eggs removed from the foster-parents among the other pairs, assuming that they have started brooding at about the same time. That's one reason accurate record keeping is so important.

The incubator can also render good service, when the female abandons the hatch unexpectedly, and this is not noticed for several hours. Cockatiel eggs can endure more than we think.

Many eggs are also lost, because the nest box is too dry, so the young hatch from the egg with difficulty and die of suffocation. To avoid this furnish the bottom layer of the nest with humid peat-moss; on top of this peat-moss we can lay coarse wood-shavings or one or more of the materials already mentioned. So you see, humidity plays a very important role in the success of a hatch. Unfortunately, it occasionally happens, that Cockatiels toss the material around in the nest or throw it out of the nest box, so that in the end the eggs will lie upon a "bone-dry" bottom after all. You can prevent this with a double floor; drill a few holes in the top floor and put a saucer of water on the bottom of the second floor. We described this idea earlier. A few damp chunks of grass sod placed in the nest box after having firmly pressed them down, can be useful, too. I prefer the first method to the second.

When the birds come out of the incubator or are abandoned by their parents, you will have to raise them yourself by handfeeding, using an eye dropper or plastic syringe. It is very important that you have enough time; it can be difficult if you are not a professional breeder and so can't be available every hour. Even those, who have the opportunity of feeding the young during the day, very seldom succeed in this. You have already scored a great success if they remain alive for 10 days, but then they often die of intestinal disturbances and similar trouble. It is currently held that the young birds should be fed with so-called crop-milk and at the moment there are a few universities investigating this scientifically.

Whether it is absolutely necessary to feed the young with crop-milk is highly doubtful however. In this context Dr. H. D. Groen notes the following in his book *Australian Parrakeets* (Haren, Holland):

If young parrots need crop-milk in the first few days to grow up in a normal way, indeed, then it stands to reason that the production of this crop-milk by the parent bird begins at the end of the brooding-period when young birds can be expected. An experience I had with Bourke's parrots clearly demonstrated, however, that this is not the case. In the nest of these Bourke's parrots a young

Red-rumped parrot was placed, that had just come out in the incubator. The female Bourke's parrot hadn't even completed her own hatch yet and had been brooding two days at the most. Nevertheless this young was accepted and already that same evening some food was visible in the youngster's crop. The next few days two more Red-rumped parrots were placed in the nest and all three parrots were not only excellently raised, but also turned out to be strong and healthy birds. So we may assume that they had no shortage of any kind during their youth. If the theory of the crop-milk is correct then this parent-bird had crop-milk at its disposal at a moment that certainly no young could be expected.

I have personally experienced a few similar cases, among others with the Cactus conure (*Aratinga cactorum*), under which two young of the Brown-throated conure (*Pyrrhura cruentata*) were placed as foster-children. In this case, too, the young were fed long before the eggs of the Cactus conure would have hatched.

In 1965, during an Australian study visit, I had a similar experience with an Elegant grass parrakeet (*Neophema elegans*) that had to care for no fewer than five young of the Turquoise parrot (*N. pulchella*) as foster-children, when she was brooding on six eggs for only four days.

So it is not altogether clear yet, what the function of crop-milk is and when exactly it is produced, but it remains a fact that young that have just hatched are raised by hand only with great difficulty even if human assistance is forthcoming at the right time. Usually it is noticed just a little too late that the female doesn't feed her youngsters anymore.

Sometimes handfeeding becomes necessary if some young are reluctant to leave the nest box, even though they are fully feathered. Mrs. Jo Hall stated in her book *Cockatiels . . . Care and Breeding* (Thorndale, Texas):

> If the female is sitting on a new clutch of eggs, she may pluck the babies to force them out of the box or the parents may quit feeding entirely those remaining in the box. I watch the youngsters closely and check their crops each evening to be sure they are full. If a youngster remains in the box and appears to be hungry or has been plucked, I take him out of the box and begin handfeeding, but I leave him in the breeding pen and, usually, the male will feed him at least part of the time until the youngster begins to eat at the feed table in the pen.

Experience, however, has taught us that we cannot feed the young by hand until they are at least 8-10 days old, as during that time the eyes will open. If, for one reason or another, the eyes don't open after 10-11 days, bathe them gently with lukewarm boric acid solution to remedy the situation.

A thin oatmeal porridge is excellent food for the first few days. We always give the food lukewarm, because the birds won't take it otherwise. We give the food with a plastic or silver teaspoon or with a plastic ear syringe. Don't use a glass syringe, as that can break too easily. (N.B. An eye or ear dropper should be used only during the first few days because it will soon become clogged when we start serving food of a heavier consistency.)

In order to feed a young Cockatiel, hold the fledgling in one hand so the head is held between thumb and index finger and use the other hand to actually feed. After each feeding clean the beak with lukewarm water and a flannel or similar soft cloth; no spilled food particles should be left on the beak or elsewhere on the bird's body. Sometimes the birds will not accept the food offered them; in that case, a little sugar added to the mixture can do wonders. Be sure to keep the crop full, but remember that filling it too much is not good either. For the first few days the fledglings will need to be fed every three hours—that is, six times a day. Night feedings are not necessary, as the female does not feed her young during the evening or night either. There is no need to sacrifice your nights to your birds!

My experience is that the best times for these six feedings are: 7 A.M., 10 A.M., 1 P.M., 4 P.M., 7 P.M., and 10 P.M. Some fanciers advise against starting before eight o'clock, but I think an early evening feeding is more wholesome than a late one. Birds need rest and investigations have proven that birds are hungrier by ten than by eleven—the hour we should have given food had we started an hour later. However, scheduling feedings is an individual matter; I only propose what I think best.

The first three feedings consist of oatmeal, possibly supplemented with honey, cane sugar, dextrose or castor sugar; the fourth and fifth feedings consist of finely crushed, ovendried bread and baby cereal in addition to the oatmeal, sugar and honey mixture. The sixth feeding should consist of just oatmeal with sugar and honey. The first day the oatmeal should be made with water; in fact, it is best not to use milk for the first five days; after that you can use both milk and water in making the porridge.

The second day dried bread and baby cereal may again be offered. After the third day we can add a little raw apple sauce to the menu, sweetened with powdered sugar and/or honey. The apple sauce should not be served too cold either, otherwise it will be refused.

On the afternoon of the fourth day, add mashed carrots, served warm; the carrots should not be boiled, however, since too much nutritional value will be lost. We can also mix in finely chopped lettuce and apple. A few drops (never more than two drops for a two ounce portion) of cod liver oil or a vitamin supplement are highly recommended.

Starting with the fifth day, add finely ground eggshell and a small amount of ground cuttlebone. It is advisable to be stingy with the latter: ½ tsp. divided between the feedings of a single day is sufficient.

Prepare all the feedings for the day in the morning, because it is practically impossible to prepare fresh food six times a day. The food should be kept in the refrigerator, to prevent deterioration. Before each "meal" the food is warmed well again. Remember, young Cockatiels are not content with cold food and will refuse it.

Theoretically, the crops of young birds should be empty after three hours. Don't worry if this isn't always so during the first few days; it is only a sign that you provided food that was too rich. Modify the diet immediately to prevent disturbances in the intestine and digestive organs. In such cases, return exclusively to oatmeal prepared with warm water for the next three days; feed this food as hot as possible! After ten days, five feedings a day can suffice, after fifteen days with four feedings, at 8 A.M., 12 noon, 4 P.M. and 8 P.M.

During the period in which the young are fed by hand, they should be housed in a spacious wooden box of 15 x 15 inches, situated in a waterproof and draftproof area.

At first only the breeder should feed the young, later his family can help. The chicks will serve notice by their call that they are hungry and want to be fed. After a few days the baby birds will be used to the feeding, and it will no longer require as much time to fill their crops. As soon as they see you coming with the food and the teaspoon they will open their beaks and the feeding will be child's play.

Incidentally, we use food syringes (available in pet stores), as the ear syringe or nose dropper can only be used during the first few days, because it can easily get clogged when feeding more substantial food.

However, you are not out of the woods yet, for soon the young Cockatiels will want their independence; they will try to get out of their box continually and will regularly refuse the food offered. At this point, put the birds in a spacious cage immediately, furnished with some well-formed wooden perches arranged so you can feed your birds with a teaspoon through the wire netting or the bars.

The growing birds will no longer be easily caught. Attempting to do so is likely to net the catcher some painful bites. Later this problem will disappear, for hand-fed Cockatiels will usually become very tame, affectionate birds.

Apart from the normal menu previously described, the young birds get a rich variety of crushed millet as well as fresh grass seed, weed seed, millet, millet spray, and canary seed on the stem. I purposely state that the seeds should be on the stem, because the birds will take the stem in their beaks and will so learn to eat the seed the natural way.

Give them extra food through the wire netting or through the bars for 14 to 20 days several times a day, and you can say your experiment—the raising of young Cockatiels—has succeeded.

Once the birds are independent, put them in a large pen (flight, aviary), so that they are able to fly; a flight of 10 feet long will be ideal. For the first few weeks make certain the birds spend the night in the shelter. That's why each aviary should have a light shelter that is higher than the run or flight, since most birds, and surely Cockatiels, prefer to sit as high as possible. When you are certain your young ones are in their shelter, the door to the flight is closed. Do not open the door again before eight o'clock in the morning. When the weather is bad, keep the birds in the shelter during the first week.

Now, let's consider the so-called "stragglers," which are sometimes found in a nest with well-fed youngsters; birds that are suddenly no longer fed by the female. Ornithologists have not yet discovered the cause of this phenomenon. Under natural conditions I have also been able to ascertain, even with various Australian parrots and parakeets, that one or more of the young are sometimes not fed any longer. So take care! Such behavior by the parents points at natural control of the species; the parents sense instinctively that there is something wrong with such stragglers and that they are thrown out of the nest or are no longer fed due to such defects. This is probably a form of culling. Step in and raise those "outcasts" yourself with the food-syringe. If the youngster is fed well for a few days he will catch up with his brothers and sisters in no time and can often be returned to the nest, where the parents will usually accept him and behave as if nothing strange has ever happened!

We have dealt in detail with the breeding and care of young birds. Perhaps you got the impression, while reading, that everything is quite easy. While approaching the project optimistically, always bear in mind, that you are working with complex, living creatures and must therefore always pay scrupulous attention to the housing, feeding and behavior of your birds. After a while you will feel almost by instinct when there is something wrong with the birds. Until you develop the knack, daily attention is not only desirable, but absolutely necessary. Everyone will agree with that.

Proper Management and Record Keeping

The necessity of banding young Cockatiels (as well as other aviary birds) as well as the records that must be kept if one wishes to breed the birds in a responsible manner, cannot be questioned. To help you a bit with the management of your Cockatiels, here are several hints. Keep a notebook and record everything important regarding your birds. Each bird should have its own section in the notebook, because over the course of time you will develop those records into a valuable reference to guide you in your breeding. By systematically keeping up the record—and this is most important—you can follow all the pairs to determine whether or not they were pure-bred, whether they were good or bad breeders, if they fed well, if they were aggressive and so forth. It is very possible that it will take several breeding seasons to build up a really comprehensive picture of all your birds.

The record can follow the plan shown below. I have taken a page from one of my own Cockatiel notebooks. You could improve, fill in or alter any part according to your own needs.

Housing:	*Ring No. of male:*	*Ring No. of female:*
Aviary 3	84-1982	76-1982
Outer coloring of male:	*Outer coloring of female:*	
Gray	Gray	

99

Ring color of male and female:
Red

Remarks: To distinguish the parents from the probable offspring, both adults wear a color ring on the right foot.

Date of Hatching of Offspring:
First brood: May 26, 1982
Second brood:
Third brood:

Ring No. of Offspring:
First brood: 98-1982; 99-1982; 100-1982; 101-1982; 102-1982.
              N.B.: No. 101-1982 died a week after leaving the nest.
Second brood:
Third brood:

Ring color of Offspring:
Blue

Color of Offspring:
First brood: 98-1982—Gray (male)
              99-1982—Gray (hen)
          100-1982—Gray (male)
          101-1982—Gray (male)
          102-1982—Gray (hen)
Second brood:
Third brood:

Special remarks:
1. Homozygous according to appearance
2. Female parent is a good breeding bird

    The use of filing cards is also good but requires a little more work. Each bird has its own card on which is listed all pertinent facts and breeding history. These cards can be stored in an index file or in boxes. You can buy the cards in any stationery store in a variety of colors and sizes or have cards cut to your own measurements.

    These cards can also be placed in a notebook. On each card for each bird the following points can be listed:

Color:	
Date of Birth:	
Color of Mother:	Color of Grandmother:
Ring No.:	Ring No.:
Color of Father:	Color of Grandfather:
Ring No.:	Ring No.:
Sex:	Special observations:
Ring No.:	
Heredity line:	

The more information recorded on the cards, the better you are able to determine the quality of the bird concerned.

If you want to sell a particular bird about which everything is known, the buyer need only check the card. He gets the card with his purchase and can continue to add notations as he continues with the breeding. Moreover, accurate card keeping can disclose a surprising picture of the bird, not only concerning its genetic properties, but also its relationship with birds of its own kind and with others, breeding performance and other important information. At the same time you can distinguish the good from the less desirable. The *good* bird should never be sold arbitrarily, but only to another devoted, enthusiastic breeder. Only those who take their Cockatiel breeding seriously can efficiently carry on the good work and keep the species and the strains from deteriorating.

A young bird has its first look at the world. *Roders*

6

Breeding Cockatiel Color Mutations

The Cockatiel has every virtue an aviculturist could wish for and not a single fault. It is easy to breed, easy to sex when adult, naturally steady, neither noisy nor destructive and does not need large or expensive accommodation.

And yet it was not until the late 1960s and the early 1970s when several mutations became generally available, that the Cockatiel began to be extensively kept in Europe, although its popularity in the USA as a pet was never in doubt.

Rosemary Low in
Parrots, Their Care and Breeding
(Blandford Press, Poole, Dorset)

SUPPOSE YOU ARE NO LONGER A BEGINNER in the Cockatiel fancy, and have graduated to the level of an experienced bird keeper. You know what your birds' housing and feeding requirements are and what to do if any of your birds should happen to become ill.

But now you have applied yourself to heredity and cross-breeding; you were convinced that you could breed a lutino male to a pied female and get lutino males and pied females, while in reality you got an offspring of normal male chicks in appearance but split for both lutino and pied, and female chicks that were lutino but also split for pied.

You were full of enthusiasm when you started experimenting, until you discovered to your utter amazement that quite a few different "results" were produced! You found this rather strange because other bird breeders seemed to know exactly what results they could expect from certain pairs of birds. This is why I would like to tell you about the more important aspects of genetics—the science of heredity.

The Miracle of Chromosomes

Every living organism is derived from a union of an egg cell (from the mother) and a sperm cell (from the father). The resulting cell formed by this union is called a *zygote* (fertilized egg cell). Once this zygote starts to develop, a certain period of time and a whole series of involved processes later, a new individual comes into existence, or for our purposes a young Cockatiel. From our school years we will probably still remember that all plants and animals, including man, are made up of millions of cells. (For simplicity's sake we will forget about the one-celled animals and plants.) All these cells originate from the zygote. To enable such a microscopic cell to "grow" there is "something" that makes this growth possible. The multiplying of the cells is caused by cell division; this, too, should ring familiar in our ears. At a given moment the zygote divides itself into two equal parts; these two parts follow suit after they have first grown into complete cells themselves (one might say they become equal again with the mother cell), and so on and so forth. In the center of the cell there is a partition that splits the cell in half. This partition only comes into existence when the two parts of such a split cell have become completely equal to each other and are virtually two completely independent cells. This partition is not really a partition in the true sense of the word, at least not with animal cells—we actually find only a construction into the cell wall—a real partition only exists with plant cells.

After several cell divisions have taken place, the zygote as a whole becomes larger (*morula, blastula,* and then *gastrula* stages). Finally the mature egg (including the white, yolk and zygote) is covered by a calcium shell for protection. If such an egg is kept within a certain temperature range for a set period of time, a bird will come out of it.

Let's go back for a minute to the single-celled zygote formed by the union of the sperm cell and the egg cell. These reproductive cells are called *gametes,* so both the sperm cell from the father and the egg cell from the mother are gametes. These gametes, then, possess all of the hereditary factors that are also present in the male and the female. In the nucleus of the cell there are small bodies, *chromosomes,* carriers of the *genes* which determine the hereditary factors. Put differently, the chromosomes are the carriers of heredity.

We just finished speaking of cell division (2, 4, 8, 16, 32, 64, 128, etc.). but if this division would continue unchecked, our Cockatiel would soon no longer fit in a cage or an aviary but would, in fact, need a large building to

104

house him! After a given period of time, even these quarters would become too tight. It is necessary, therefore, that an organism regulate its growth and at a certain point cease further growth and become occupied with body maintenance.

The mechanism that does this consists of small parts in the innermost section of the cell which can only be seen under the microscope. This miracle of almost indescribable technique has within it still smaller bodies, called *genes,* which determine hereditary characteristics, such as color. You may be aware of the fact that every cell possesses an even number of chromosomes, so when the cell is split in half, the chromosomes also split in two, so that each divided cell possesses the same number of divided chromosomes. Once cell division has taken place, the chromosomes will once again regain their original "unsplit" size.

But Nature also has its exceptions. We can find this with the first reproductive cells which can unite to form a new cell. The reproductive cells have only half of each of the total number of chromosomes, as already mentioned. To make things a little clearer, example is here offered. Suppose the cells have eighteen chromosomes (as, for example, with the Canary); the egg cell will have contributed nine chromosomes, as will the sperm cell. When these two cells unite upon fertilization and form a zygote, it is obvious that this zygote carries nine chromosomes from the sperm cell and nine from the egg cell. If we add these up, then we have eighteen chromsomes again. This splitting of the total number of chromosomes into two groups with half the original number is called *reduction division.* When this zygote, possessing eighteen chromosomes, divides, the normal cell division will take place, as discussed before. In other words, we will then get 2, 4, 8, 16, 32, 64, 128, 256, 512 cells ad infinitum, each of which will always retain eighteen chromosomes. Research has shown that man has 46 chromosomes. So man has 46 chromosomes per cell, or 23 pairs.

The zygote receives nine chromosomes from the egg cell and nine chromosomes from the sperm cell. We already know that the chromosomes are the carriers of the hereditary factors (coloring, outer appearance, character and others), so we can now see that a young Cockatiel will inherit characteristics from both the mother and the father. Later we will discuss a few exceptions to this under *Sex-Linked Heredity,* where special factors are inherited only by the male offspring or only by the female offspring.

Chromosomes possess genes that are the determining factors regarding the inherited characteristics of the new organism. The young Cockatiel receives half of these from the father and half from the mother, since the young bird also receives half the amount of genes (reduction division) from each parent. The young bird therefore gets the hereditary factors from both parents. This does not imply that a crossing of white x dark gray, as an example, will produce all light gray offspring, since we have yet to direct our attention to the hidden and visible factors which are called recessive and dominant factors respectively. Both factors are extremely important to the heredity of Cockatiels, since a certain color may very well dominate another color. From the example given above (which is not necessarily an established crossing, but only used to illustrate a point), it is entirely possible that there will be white and dark gray offspring as well as light gray in the nest. However, I am sure everyone will agree that the majority of the color mutations known in Cockatiels are far from dominant to the wild color; in fact they are what is called recessive. In other words when a Cockatiel of a certain color (all but the wild color) is paired to gray or wild color mate the offspring look exactly like wild color phase with not even a slight indication that one of the parents was a different color.

This does not mean that a gray bird carries no other color; in fact, a certain percentage is very likely to possess "color" genes, except that they are not visible, so the gray birds very likely do have some other mutated color, but this cannot be seen with the naked eye. After all, the offspring had both gray and mutated color passed down to them from their parents.

Certain circumstances may arise where a certain factor (in this case the color factor) gets the upper hand, pushing another factor to the side in favor of itself. A color originates from the gene. The father or the mother may have a white gene and a dark green gene, as an example, and now the question is which of these two factors, these two colors if you prefer, will dominate, which one will be visible in the baby bird. The invisible color is "inside the bird," hidden in the genes, but it is nevertheless present in the baby bird.

Recessive and Dominant Factors

When we know some of the terms used in genetics (the science of heredity), such as zygote, genes and chromosomes, we are ready to broaden our knowledge on this subject. We know that a bird has an exterior coloring, which may or may not be passed on to its offspring. We spoke of an example using a crossing of white x dark gray. I would like to point out again that the offspring are not necessarily going to reveal a combination of both colors. This is because the parent birds also possess hidden color genes, the invisible factors called *recessive factors*. A visible factor, as already mentioned, is known as the *dominant factor*.

Sex-Linked Heredity

You will very likely have concluded from the above that the sex of each offspring is determined by the genes. The female Cockatiel has two sex-determining chromosomes, namely one X chromosome or male chromosome and one Y chromosome or female chromosome. The male also has two sex-determining chromosomes, but both of his are X chromosomes . . . the male chromosome. The sexual difference between the male and female then lies in the fact that the female has both a male and female chromosome, while the
106

male has two identical male X chromosomes. (This explanation is simpler, though less accurate than saying the Y chromosome indicates an absence of a male sex chromosome, rather than calling it a female sex chromosome.) In a diagram we can clarify this as follows:

(cock or male) X chromosome x (hen or female) X chromosome = 2 x X chromosomes = male.

Assuming that you fully understand everything so far, let's make tracks and cover some more ground in this jungle of theory. First we will make the possibly astounding statement that both a heterozygous and a homozygous Cockatiel could be identical in appearance. A homozygous gray bird possesses only the color gray, while a bird of impure heredity may be gray (in lesser or greater degree) externally but in addition possess other (internal) colors. In short, it possesses the tendency to pass on another color (often unknown to us) to its offspring. I said "unknown" because, while the parents of this heterozygous bird were gray, they also possess hidden colors since they were not pure-bred. (These young birds are heterozygous, having two different genes [or *allelomorphs*], where dominant and recessive genes are both present for any trait or traits. A homozygous individual is pure for a given trait, possessing matched genes for that trait; the opposite of heterozygous.) It would follow that when we cross two homozygous birds (that is, homozygous for the same color) we can also expect pure-bred offspring. Gray x gray (both homozygous) produces 100% gray cocks and gray hens; this cannot vary, since the parent birds cannot transmit a color that they do not possess themselves. The parents are pure-bred and therefore will breed true to their own characteristics. The young, in their turn, will also breed 100% true to character.

Mutations

Mutation is a word you will come across frequently in any discussion of heredity. When a sudden change takes place in the color or form of an organism which cannot be explained genetically, the phenomenon is termed a mutation. Through unexplained changes in the hereditary composition of the chromosomes, sudden changes in color and/or form can appear. Sometimes these changes can be purposely brought about, but with amateur breeders it is usually a spontaneous and sudden thing. How lucky we are when a desirable mutation happens!

Mutation should not be confused with modification. The latter represents something quite different. By serving feeds having certain chemical activities in them or, even more often, are lacking in certain elements (particularly vitamins and minerals), changes or modifications can be brought about, but these changes will disappear again when the feeding is back to normal. For example, the intense red coloring of the red-orange Canary is largely achieved by adding carrot juice or other chemicals to its water or by giving it other food preparations that will enhance color.

107

Mutations can be, and often are, inheritable. This is the major difference from modifications, where genetics plays no role at all, since the changes were artificially brought about.

In addition, inbreeding will often be necessary in the case of mutations. This means that the mutant will have to be crossed back to its father or mother in an attempt to produce more individuals which exhibit the same mutated characteristics. The parents of a mutation are not, of course, both responsible for its appearance, at least in most cases. If the mutant is a hen and the father can be established as being responsible for the mutation, then it will only take one round of inbreeding (father x daughter) to reproduce the trait. If, however, the mother can be determined as being the cause of the mutation, it will take two rounds of inbreeding: first we cross-breed father x daughter, and a son from this union is then inbred with the first hen, i.e. grandmother x grandson. You will see that the second round will produce more mutants. Under these circumstances, inbreeding can be very useful, even necessary; under different circumstances, however, it is not very advisable, at least if we want to prevent our bird population from degenerating into a weakened strain.

Genes

In a zygote 50% of the chromosomes come from each parent. In Cockatiels, the cock has nine pairs of chromosomes, but the hen also has nine pairs; if the zygote received nine pairs from both parents, it would have 18 pairs, and of course that would not be possible. This is where reduction-division comes into play, the division of the sex cells (*diploid cells* or cells with chromosome pairs from which *haploid reproductive cells* or gametes originate through reduction division). This division implies that all of the chromosomes are halved, with the baby bird then possessing nine pairs. The chromosomes hold the genes (in single form) which possess the heredity factors.

Lethal Factors

Certain gene combinations are not or barely viable; in other words, they can be lethal to the sex cells, zygote, embryo (the young life inside the egg), or to the newly hatched chick. I will warn you of the lethal factor wherever this applies in our descriptions of the color mutations.

Mendel's Theory

Whenever we speak of heredity and crossing, we frequently use the word *Mendelian.* Any knowledgeable bird breeder can tell you that this word comes from Gregor Mendel, the name of the priest-biologist who experimented primarily with plants and flowers. But who was he actually?

108

Gregor Johann Mendel was born in Heizendorf, Austria in 1822. When he was 21 he entered the Augustinian Monastery at Brünn (Brno, Czechoslovakia), where he was ordained a priest in 1847. From 1851 to 1853 he studied natural science in Vienna and then returned to the monastery. In 1868 he was appointed abbot of his monastery, where he continued his experiments for many years. When he died in 1884 he was honored as a fine abbot, but was completely unknown as a scientist who laid the foundation for the whole theory of heredity. Only years later was the intrinsic value of his work appreciated and recognized.

Mendel started his experiments in 1865 with the common garden pea. He chose this legume because it had the advantage of providing a great number of seedlings in each generation and he could accurately observe the relationship between the various types and their hereditary factors. By pollenating two like plants himself, he could tell whether the new plant that appeared was pure-bred or not.

Mendel published his research and discoveries in publications of the Brünn Society for the Study of Natural Science in 1865, but it was not until 1900 that De Vries of the Netherlands, Tschermak of Austria and Correns of Germany discovered Mendel's work and gave it the prominence and appreciation it deserved.

Briefly stated, here are the Mendel's laws:

1. In principle the male and female sex cells are especially equipped to pass on hereditary characters, which means that it makes no difference if a particular character comes from the mother or the father.

2. The sex cells are pure-bred and therefore cannot possess a deviating character. In other words, when the sex cells divide they do not contain pairs of chromosomes. They have only one chromosome from each pair. One sperm cell or one egg cell can pass on only one character from each pair of chromosomes.

3. Heredity embraces a number of tendencies (the Danish plant expert Johannsen, 1857-1927, spoke of genes in connection with this) that work independently of one another.

Meanwhile the terms "lutino," "opaline," "cinnamon," "pied" and other mutations actually mean genetically *pure* color mutations. In other words, we are speaking of colored birds that we know to be homozygous, pure-bred for a particular character. On the other hand, if a heterozygous (not pure-bred) bird is bred for a particular quality, then for the sake of convenience it is listed by the visible color as well as its recessive or invisible color. A heterozygous bird that is outwardly gray but carries pied would be classified as a gray/pied bird or a "gray-blooded" Cockatiel, which means that gray is dominant and pied is recessive (and not visible). No matter what we call it, the meaning is now clear. The different names can easily lead to confusion, so I will stick to the terminology generally used in bird breeding literature—the English term *split*. In our example then, we have gray split for pied (gray/pied).

Champions Through Selection

If you visit a bird show, you will find that birds are not classified by color alone but by their form and condition as well. A breeder who is sloppy in his work will not get very far. His dreams of success will never materialize, and his birds will degenerate into pathetic, little feathered lumps. The breeder whose main object is to breed as many birds as possible regardless of color, form or condition will discover that after he reaches his objective his birds will only be unsuitable breeding material that even the inexperienced beginner will shy away from. The sincere breeder will not rest before being able to breed *choice* birds. He or she can rightly ask a fair price for birds of good breeding and will resolutely back the birds' quality.

How does one arrive at that point? Not surprisingly, the best guarantee of good birds is the rigorously carried-through, yearly selection process. Throughout this book the greatest emphasis has already been placed upon the importance of having good pairs in prime condition. Sick birds needing medication may recover but will not be of first quality color, condition and form. Such Cockatiels are good for keepers who are only interested in raising birds as a sort of sport or hobby but have no intention of exhibiting or breeding for profit. It is best to spend the first few years breeding Cockatiels for fine condition and then concentrate on color.

The second possibility to try, once you have healthy quality birds, is to breed Cockatiels with precisely the same heredity pattern that the breeder has worked out. You cannot do this yourself until you have worked out your own routine. This routine is completely relative, in view of the fact that experienced bird breeders must struggle with the same difficulties as the beginner; namely, determining which hereditary factors went into producing those good, healthy birds. Luck plays a big part in this because the chances of acquiring a purely descended (homozygous) pair are rather remote. When you think you have finally gotten such a couple, after several broods you may look in the nest and suddenly discover that there are babies in there with strange colors that were never observed either in the mother or father. If you have impurely (heterozygous) descended Cockatiels, this can be remedied and is certainly no reason to give up bird breeding and keeping.

To get the most purely bred Cockatiels possible, you may work with only one color or with more than one color as long as each is kept completely separated from the others in an aviary, for example, wild color with wild color, lutino with lutino and cinnamon with cinnamon. If you immediately start breeding with different mutations together in one aviary, you will get a variegated collection of colors and miscolors and have nothing to continue with.

Very often the breeder cannot tell from the outward appearance of a Cockatiel whether a bird is a completely pure (homozygous) color or a genetic mutation. Some birds may not possess any observable identifying marks (they are said to be *split,* as you know, for such a marking), which may well become

110

visible later in the next offspring. He must therefore keep on top of the situation. When he knows that his cinnamon Cockatiels breed pure cinnamon, then it is simple to follow the rules of heredity we have learned— that the crossing of a cinnamon with a cinnamon give cinnamon young. By ringing particular colors you can easily distinguish the offspring from other birds. You can understand how important this is if you wish to breed further. It is also an exacting science to achieve success in the breeding of other color variations and mutations.

It was mentioned earlier that gray (pure gray or wild color) sometimes becomes inbred. When you are sure that you have a pure, wild gray Cockatiel and you want to breed it with another color, there is no cause for concern. The new issue will be just as described herein. On the other hand, if you have *impurely* bred wild colored Cockatiels, you may get later generations with colors that do not belong at all with the expected color or mutation.

In order to get a pure breeding stock, you must keep the birds separated by color (mutation). The impure offspring that can appear from various crossings (such as white young with gray in their feathers) are then removed. In the long run this is how you get a homozygous white breeding stock. Naturally the parents are removed because, as seen from their offspring, they are not pure-bred. With this process you develop a strain that is pure white genetically and externally. Needless to say, this does not happen in short order and certainly not if you first have to seek out the homozygous birds from all the birds you have. Those of pure white descent may be among the younger as well as the older birds. You can avoid these difficulties if you buy homozygous individuals from a reliable breeder. There is no doubt that it can be very interesting to try to build up your own stock with identical heredity factors, even if it does take a long time. You will probably have to pay a breeder a bit more, but later on you can ask a fine price for your own pure-bred offspring. Be thoroughly aware that such birds are not to be exploited. Use them sparingly and leave the experimenting to those who raise birds only for profit.

Genetics and Color Breeding

All living organisms are, as we have already seen in the previous pages, composed of a great number of minute units, called cells. Each cell has a nucleus, a "brain center" that contains threadlike bodies called chromosomes, which hold many particles known as genes. Diploid cells have these chromosomes in pairs, the members of which are homologous, so that twice the haploid number is present. Hence "haploid" means: having a single set of un-paired, not matching chromosomes in each nucleus. During fertilization each egg cell and sperm cell bring forth a haploid set of chromosomes, therefore a zygote or fertilized egg cell has again a complete set of diploid chromosomes, and after each cell division every cell will have diploid chromosomes.

111

In a mutation we may, for instance, find a gene for white on one chromosome, instead of the expected gene for gray. In practice it becomes apparent that many color mutations inherit recessives in connection with the dominant wild or gray color.

A recessive color is, as we have also seen, not visible.

In regard to these remarks, and as it also applies to the rules of dominant and recessive inheritance, consider the following example:

A crossing between a homozygous gray male Cockatiel (GG) and a homozygous white female (ww) gives 100% gray/white offspring. Before I explain how we arrive at this, note that capital letters (GG) are used to symbolize dominant factors (colors); small letters (ww) indicate recessives.

In the first generation (called "F₁"—F stands for *filius* or son) all the young are gray in color, exactly like the father, as gray is a dominant color. In other words: by crossing two birds that are homozygous the young (the F₁) will naturally be homozygous as well.

In our example, however, we are mating two birds with two different colors: gray and white. The offspring is so-called "split," as the young receive the gray dominant color (G) from the father, and the white, recessive color (w) from the mother. This outcome is written as "gray/white" (Gw). In appearance (phenotype) all the young are gray, like their father, but they also received the invisible white color from their mother. The young birds are gray in appearance, but possess the white color too. The offspring are gray, but split for white (genotype). In an outline we see it this way:

1) Parents or P-generation

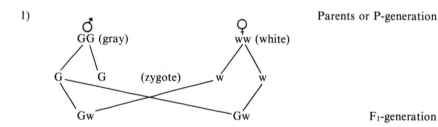

By a crossing Gw x Gw the outcome is:

2)

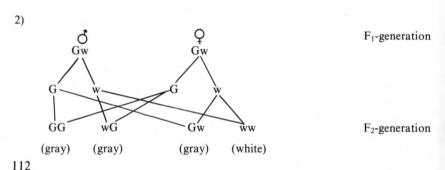

112

Or:

♀\♂	G	w
G	GG	Gw
w	Gw(=wG)	ww

1 x GG

1 x ww

1 x Gw

= 1 : 1 : 2

We see that 50% of the zygote have the gene G and 50% the gene w. The phenotype in the F_2-generation gives a proportion of 3 : 1; in other words three birds are gray and one is white. The genotype is 1 : 2 : 1, or 25% of the offspring is homozygous for gray, 50% is gray/white (gray in appearance but white recessive; split for white), and 25% is homozygous white. So only in the second generation (F_2) we will, at last, get what we are aiming for, namely 25%. In order to obtain more white Cockatiels we must cross-breed with one of the parents of the first generation (F_1):

3)

Gw (gray)   ww (white)

Or:

♀\♂	G	w
w	Gw	ww
w	wG (= Gw)	ww

2 x Gw

2 x ww

= 1 : 1

Here we get the following results: 50% gray/white (split for white) and 50% homozygous white.

The following Cockatiel-mutations are recessive for gray:
1. white, with black eyes
2. pied, with black eyes
3. pearled, with black eyes

113

4. diluted
5.* fawn or cinnamon

Here sex does not play any part in the outcome of the color.

The percentage only makes good sense if you figure on a large scale of 100 birds. It is quite common that in the first nest all the young are gray, split for white, and in the second nest all homozygous recessive.

Our first and third crossing are, as you will understand, very important, but so is a crossing of two homozygous recessive Cockatiels, as we can define the descendants immediately with regard to their inherited factors.

We already know that in each nucleus there are, next to the chromosomes, two so-called sex-determining chromosomes: XX for a male; XY for a female. We call the X-chromosome a "male chromosome," the Y-chromosome a "female-chromosome;" as you know too the Y-chromosome determines the sex of the bird.

There are quite a few color-mutations that have sex-linked inheritance; in other words the gene for a certain factor is situated on the X-chromosome.

As females possess only one X-chromosome they always inherit homozygous traits. Males however can be split for a certain mutation when only one X-chromosome (they have two X-chromosomes) carries the color gene. Due to the fact that the other X-chromosome carries the wild color gene (gray), which is dominant, the other X-chromosome will be, as it were, "pushed into the background."

For instance: a crossing of an albino male x gray female gives:

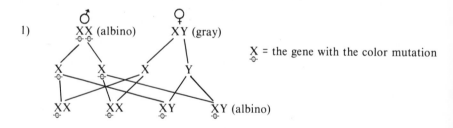

1) ♂ XX (albino)   ♀ XY (gray)

X = the gene with the color mutation

XX   XX   XY   XY (albino)

Or:

♀ \ ♂	X	X
X	XX	XX
Y	XY	XY

2 x XX = albino females

2 x XY = gray/albino males

Gray male (XX) x albino female (XY):

2)

♀ \ ♂	X	X
X̶	X̶X	X̶X
Y	XY	XY

2 x X̶X   all young are gray
2 x XY

Split male (XX) x gray female (XY):

3)

♀ \ ♂	X	X̶
X	XX	X̶X
Y	XY	X̶Y

1 x XX

1 x X̶X

1 x XY

1 x X̶Y (albino)

50% of the males are gray
50% of the males are split
50% of the females are gray
50% of the females are albino

Yet another example:

From our second (2) outline we take a male from the F_1-generation and cross him back with his mother: X̶X (gray) x XY (albino)

4)

♀ \ ♂	X	X̶
X	XX	X̶X
Y	XY	X̶Y

1 x XX

1 x X̶X

1 x XY

1 x X̶Y

50% of the males are gray split
50% of the males are albino
50% of the females are gray
50% of the females are albino.

Practice has proven that the crossings, given in the outlines 1 and 4, are preferred, which in this case means that the young (F_1) from outline 1 are crossed with each other. In both outlines, however, the hereditary qualities of all the young are easily determined.

Outline 2 doesn't give young of the desired color-variation, so one is again forced to cross a split male with an albino hen (outline #4). Crossing #4 is preferred, as all young are very strong physically. Next to gray (wild color) hens and split males, we also get birds of both sexes in the desired color varieties.

The following color-mutative males are sex-linked:
1. albino (white with red eyes);
2. lutinos (yellow with red eyes);
3. black-eyed pearled.

It is important to realize that pied Cockatiels inherit only partially-dominant. That is the reason why—in the first generation (F_1)—there will appear quite often the so-called "pied-heads" in a crossing between wild color (gray) x pied. These are birds that look like gray Cockatiels, but have white spots on head, neck, and on the wings. By crossing two "pied-heads," the majority of the offspring will be pied.

With the given outlines one can work out all recessive as well as all sex-linked mutations.

The Chemistry of Color

There are, as we already know, quite a few color mutations of the Cockatiel at the present time. In their feathers these birds possess the following pigments:
1. black eumelanin;
2. red carotene;
3. yellow carotene.

There are two types of melanins or "pigment grains":
1. globular grains (phaeomelanin) and
2. rod-like particles (eumelanin).

The chemical structure of the carotenes is still unknown. The gradation of the gray color depends on the strength of the eumelanin concentration in the feather-barbs and barbules.

It is therefore understandable that the stronger the concentration the darker the gray color. Research has proven that a presence of eumelanin in barbs and barbules does not necessarily mean that there will be no carotene; both (eumelanin and carotene) can be present, although if there is a strong concentration of eumelanin, carotene will become invisible.

Male Cockatiels have a strong concentration of eumelanin in the wing coverts but, a somewhat lesser concentration in the breast and belly feathers; therefore these feathers are lighter in color.

116

Hen Cockatiels possess a weaker concentration of eumelanin (dimorphism). In the barbs and barbules of the breast and belly feathers there is yellow carotene; and in case of a weak melanin concentration in breast and belly, a vague yellow hue becomes visible.

The distribution of carotene differs in male and hen. There is almost no carotene in the body feathers of the male, while in the mask of both sexes the carotene distribution as well as the concentration are alike. The "dirty" yellow color of the hen's mask is caused by the presence of black eumelanin in the barbs and barbules of the mask and crest feathers, while in the male those feathers do not contain eumelanin. Therefore the clear yellow color is obtained.

In the cheek-barbs of both sexes there is a mixture of red and yellow carotene; hence the orange color.

In some males the tip of the cheek-barbs are, for about 1 mm in length, colorless, followed by a deep orange-red, then a light orange, and finally a yellow area. So the base of each barb appears to be yellow.

The color of the cheek depends upon the following factors:

1. the length of the colorless barb-tip. The shorter the tip the more intense the color will be; the longer the tip, the duller the color.
2. Looking at the mixture red-yellow carotene, one might notice that the orange color of the cheek becomes darker when the red-component is dominant, lighter when the yellow-component is dominant.

By comparing different Cockatiels it becomes obvious that the concentration of the yellow carotene in the body feathers as well as those in the cheeks may vary considerably with each bird. Only where there is carotene present, but it is masked by melanin, will it be extremely difficult to notice.

It is a well-known fact that the yellow color of the hen's mask is due to the presence of carotene. This however does not tell us how much carotene there will be. Therefore we should look at the tail-feathers of the hen, although even here the yellow color may vary substantially. It is best to only breed from hens that have a deep yellow color.

The distribution of carotene in the male is mostly concentrated in the mask, his crest, and secondary tail-feathers. Some males show a weak carotene distribution in breast and belly feathers, but usually this will be masked through a stronger concentration of eumelanin in those particular feather parts.

The cheeks of both male and female are the same in size and similar in strength as far as the carotene concentration is concerned, but by closer observation however, one will notice that the small feathers on the outside borders of the hen's cheeks possess black eumelanin, which in turn masks the carotene present. Therefore the cheeks of a hen look smaller than those of the male. Only through the cancellation of the melanin (as is the case in the so-called Ino-Cockatiels, is the real size of the hen's cheek shown.

There is almost no carotene in the feathers of back and wings, in both male and female. But there are some exceptions, as I have seen hens with a very weak yellow carotene concentration in the white of their shoulder-patches.

Conformation and Type

The Cockatiel gives the impression of being a robust bird. Due to the rather long, pointed tail and the raised crest the bird looks slender.

The average sizes are:

Total length: 12-13 inches (30-33 cm.)

Length wings: 6-7 inches (15-17 cm.)

Length tail: 6-7 inches (15-17 cm.)

The length of the tail is half the length of the body. The term "slender" doesn't mean that the bird is shapeless. Some Cockatiels are indeed shapeless, but this is due to the small breast. In relation to the width of the head and the length of the body (without the tail), the breast must be fairly wide. It is the breast that gives the bird its format and type. The wings must meet just an inch or so over the upper tail-feathers. Crossed or drooping wings are a defect.

The Cockatiel has four toes on each foot; two in front, two behind (like a capital X).

The tail has two clearly prolonged central feathers (the so-called tail-feathers).

Cockatiels have a raised crest that tapers on top.

The upper mandible forms, together with the skull, one flowing line. The lower mandible is somewhat shorter than the upper one.

Normal Gray (or Wild Color) Cockatiel

Cock:

Body: various shades of gray, with the darkest tones being on the underside of the tail, and with the two central tail feathers being the palest shade of gray.

Front of head, cheeks, and throat are lemon yellow.

The crest is a mixture of yellow and gray, and is curved outward. Approximate length: 1 in. to 1¼ in. (2.5-3 cm).

The sides of the crown are white.

The ear patches are a mixture of red and orange; size approximately ⅝ of an inch.

Each wing has a broad white bar, tinted with pale yellow. This bar runs from the shoulder across the secondary wing coverts. Any black markings on the wings are defects. The primaries are darker gray in color.

Eyes: dark brown.

Beak: dark gray.
Feet and legs: gray; nails black.

Hen:

Body: much like the cock, but less pure (a faint brownish wash), while the ear patches may vary in size. Hens are generally not as rich in color as males. The wing bars are less pure in color.
No white on the crown. The faint yellow areas are mixed with more gray. The thighs are barred with pale yellow.
Underside tail is striped and dappled with yellow and gray.
Fully matured hens are often difficult to distinguish from first year cocks, as are fawn females.

"Black" Cockatiel

A slate-blue Cockatiel, obtained through selection. The cock has a yellow head, red cheeks and white wing bars.
The hen is darker slate-blue, without any brown markings; she resembles the gray hen.

"Green" Cockatiel

A "black" Cockatiel with a yellow head, olive-green colors on breast, wings and trunk. This mutation (a male) was first bred by a Mr. F. E. Kaedig (Hanover, Germany).
It is possible that the optical impression of the olive-green color in the feathers is caused through the influence of extra black eumelanin. Hence: yellow + gray = olive-green. Yellow + black = olive-green.

Fawn (Cinnamon or Isabella) Cockatiel

A sex-linked mutation. Young birds have reddish-colored eyes during the first few weeks.
Fawn Cockatiels are so-called white ground birds; the name "fawn" is correct, just like the term "fawn" is correctly used for Zebra finches and Canaries, where a white ground color is also involved.

Cock:

The main body color is gray-brown in various shades; the deepest tones being on the underside of the long pointed tail, and the two central feathers being of the palest shade.
The front of the head, the cheek and the throat are lemon yellow.
The crest is a mixture of yellow and grayish-brown.
The sides of the crown are white.
The ear patches are red-orange.

119

A broad white bar on each wing, tinted with some pale yellow running from the shoulders across the secondary wing-coverts.

Eyes: dark brown.

Beak: dark gray.

Feet and legs: pinkish.

Hen:

Like the cock. The ear patches are not so extensive or as rich in color. The wing bars are less pure in color.

No white on the crown; yellow areas are faintly tinted, and are more grayish-brown.

The thighs are barred with yellow.

The underside of the tail is striped and dappled with yellow and grayish-brown.

Tables

1. Fawn cock x Gray hen = Gray/fawn cocks and Fawn hens.

2. Gray cock x Fawn hen = Gray/fawn cocks and Gray hens.

3. Gray/fawn cock x Fawn hen = 50% Fawn cocks and hens.
   50% Gray/fawn cocks and Gray hens.

4. Gray/fawn cock x Gray hen = 75% Gray, of which half
   the cocks are split for Fawn, but these males cannot be distinguished from the homozygous Gray cocks.
   25% Fawn hens.

Note: Mating 4 is NOT advisable.

Dilute (or Silver) Cockatiel

Quite often domesticated birds will produce a dilute mutation. The coloring is visible only in varying degrees at less than full strength. The dilute mutation is recessive: both male and female can be split for the trait, and a pair of dilute birds will produce only dilute young. A split dilute pair gives 25% dilute young in both sexes. Of the wild (gray) colored offspring only the males are split for silver. Due to lethal factors split x silver is NOT advisable, and in such a crossing the sex is irrelevant.

Cock:

The main body color is various shades of bright silver-gray. Deeper tones on the underside of the tail, and with the two central feathers being the palest.

The front of the head, cheeks and throat are lemon-yellow.

The crest is a mixture of yellow and silvery-gray.

120

The sides of the crown are white.

The ear patches are red-orange.

There is a broad white bar on each wing. Each bar is tinted with pale yellow running from the shoulders across the secondary wing-coverts.

Eyes: reddish-brown.

Beak: gray.

Feet and legs: pinkish.

Hen:

Body color is similar to that of the cock.

Ear patches not so extensive or as rich in color.

The wing bars are less pure in color.

No white on the crown; yellow areas faintly tinted, and more silvery-gray in shade.

The thighs are barred with yellow.

The underside of the tail is striped and dappled with yellow and silver-gray.

Pearled Cockatiel

A sex-linked mutation. Due to the intensity of the color one can distinguish golden and silver pearled Cockatiels. "Golds" have only yellow on head and tail. The males have pearl-white markings, except on the wing bars, which are tinted with pale yellow.

The best crossings are gold x gold or gold x silver.

The mating silver x silver is NOT advisable.

The expectations for the pearled matings can be worked out by adapting the rules for albino matings which appear later in this section.

Cock:

The main body color is like a gray Cockatiel, but with large areas of the wing feathers "having two shades of gray coloring, making a definite, attractive pattern combination. This pattern on the wings is very much like that of the opaline Budgerigar, and like them is variable in its markings, and the sex-linked nature of its inheritance."

The orange-red color of the ear patches and the yellow suffusion on various areas do not seem to be quite so intense as on the normal gray color.

Eyes: clear brown.

Beak: gray.

Feet and legs: differing tones of gray, "sometimes with a pinkish undertone."

(C. Rogers)

Hen:

Body much like that of the male.
The ear patches are not as extensive or as rich.
The wing bars are less pure in color.
No white on the crown; the yellow areas fainter.
The thighs are barred with pale yellow.
Underside of tail is striped and dappled with clear yellow and gray.

Pied Cockatiel

Pied is recessive, and can be carried by other colors, both in males and hens in split form.

Cock:

Body similar to gray, with irregular shaped white or yellow tinted white patches of varying size.
Eyes: dark brown.
Beak: dark gray.
Feet and legs: gray, pinkish, or a mixture of both.

Hen:

Like gray (wild color) hen, but with the plumage broken by irregular shaped white and yellow-tinted white patches of varying size.

Tables

RECESSIVE PIED NORMAL GRAY INHERITANCE

1. Pied Gray x Gray =
   100% Gray/pied for cocks and hens.

2. Pied Gray x Gray/pied =
   50% Gray/pied cocks and hens
   50% Pied Gray cocks and hens.

3. Gray/pied x Gray/pied =
   25% Gray cocks and hens.
   50% Gray/pied cocks and hens.
   25% Pied Gray cocks and hens.

4. Gray/pied x Gray =
   50% Gray cocks and hens.
   50% Gray/pied cocks and hens.

5. Pied Gray x Pied Gray =
   100% Pied Gray cocks and hens.

122

It is immaterial which member of a pair is pied gray or the split color. C. Rogers stated correctly that "to maintain and improve a stud of pied normal grays it is essential that the normal gray/pieds be used regularly in the pairing. The best results are obtained when the "split" birds are from the crossing of normal gray to pied normal gray. This rule applies to all color matings where "split" birds are used. Birds from such crossings are known as first cross Splits."

And he continues: "At the beginning of this chapter, I said that the clear light areas vary in their extent; bearing this in mind it may be possible by selective pairing to produce actual clear white, but non-albino birds. Some breeders have already discovered that by mating together birds with the largest clear areas they have bred young with even greater expanses of light feathers. After a number of generations of this selective pairing it may well be that the desired objective of clear white birds could be reached. From this it will be seen that the breeding of pieds can be of great interest to the keen experimental breeder. There can also be pied in the other color forms."

White With Black Eyes

This is a recessive, and an extremely rare mutation. These white birds resemble albinos but actually have dark brown eyes, which, at first glance, however, appear black.

A mating of a gray (wild colored) male x a white (with black eyes) hen gives 100% gray young, all of which are split for white with black eyes. Hence:

White x white = 100% White.

White x split = 50% White and 50% split.

Split x split = 25% White; 25% gray (homozygous) and 50% split. This last crossing is NOT advisable.

The same rules apply for dilute Cockatiels, as this mutation is recessive. It is immaterial which member of a pair is white or split color.

Albino and "Lutino"

As albino is a sex-linked mutation, a mating of an albino cock x gray hen always gives gray males and albino hens. The same applies for fawn and pearled Cockatiels.

"Lutinos" have an extra yellow, so-called "fat-color" in the feathers of head, crest, and tail, and therefore are darker yellow than albinos.

Cock:

The body is pure white.

The front of the head, part of the cheeks, and the throat are lemon-yellow.

The crest is a mixture of yellow and white.
The ear patches are (normal) red-orange.
The wings have yellow areas.
The tail has a yellow wash.
Eyes: red.
Beak: yellow horn color.
Feet and legs: pinkish.

Hen:

Body color is the same as for the cock.
Yellow wash on the thighs and under the tail.

Tables

RULES OF SEX-LINKED ALBINO INHERITANCE

1. Albino cock x Gray hen =
   50% Gray/albino cocks.
   50% Albino hens (homozygous).

But:

2. Gray cock x Albino hen =
   50% Gray/albino cocks.
   50% Gray hens (homozygous).

3. Gray/albino cock x Albino hen =
   50% Albino (both sexes).
   50% Gray (of which the cocks are split for albino; the hens are homozygous gray).

4. Gray/Albino cock x Gray hen =
   25% Gray cocks.
   25% Gray hens.
   25% Gray/albino cocks.
   25% Albino hens.

5. Albino cock x Albino hen =
   100% Albino cocks and hens.

The same rules apply for fawn and pearled Cockatiels.

Some Color Varieties

Silver x Silver =
   100% Silver.

124

1.0 Silver x 0.1 Fawn =
Gray/silver/fawn cocks.
Gray/silver hens.

1,0 Fawn x 0.1 Silver =
Gray/silver/fawn cocks
Fawn/silver hens.

1,0 Fawn/silver x 0.1 Fawn/silver =
75% Fawn/silver in both sexes.
25% Fawn (Isabelle) in both sexes!

1,0 Gray/silver and Fawn x 0.1 Fawn/silver =
50% Fawn, of which half split for Silver.
25% Gray, of which half split for Silver, and the cocks split for Fawn.
12.5% Silver, of which the cocks split for Fawn.
12.5% Fawn (Isabelle) homozygous!

Hence: Fawn x Fawn = 100% Fawn.

Note: 1.0 = Cock, male;
0.1 = Hen, female;
Gray = Wild color
1 = split.

1,0 Fawn x 0.1 Gold pearled =
Gray cocks, split for Fawn and pearled
Fawn hens (homozygous).
Note: these hens are NOT recommended for further breeding in this line!

1.0 Gold pearled x 0.1 Fawn =
Gray cocks, split for Fawn and pearled.
Fawn hens (homozygous).

1.0 Gray/Fawn + Pearled x 0.1 Fawn =
Gray cocks and hens.
Fawn cocks and hens.
25% Pearled hens (at the most!) of which some (due to so-called crossing-over) are *Fawn pearled!*
The gray cocks are split for fawn, and half of them are split for pearled.
Also the fawn cocks are split. The gray hens (homozygous) can never have the fawn factor.

But:

1.0 Fawn pearled x 0.1 Fawn =
75% Fawn cocks and hens, but the cocks are split for pearled.

There is considerable interest in color mutations in the Cockatiel and many have taken up the hobby of breeding for existing mutations and developing new ones. This group includes several of the mutations that have been developed from the original gray color.

Photo by Kelley, from ALL ABOUT THE PARROTS, © 1980 by Arthur Freud and reproduced with the permission of the publisher, Howell Book House Inc.

Because Cockatiels are now bred in a variety of interesting mutations, their appeal for fanciers and pet lovers is much heightened through their beauty and intrinsic charm.   *Courtesy Ruth Hanessian*

25% Fawn pearled hens!

1.0 Fawn pearled x 0.1 Fawn pearled =
    50% Fawn cocks and hens; the cocks are split for pearled.
    50% Fawn pearled cocks and hens.

Hence: Fawn pearled x Fawn pearled =
    100% Fawn pearled.

1,0 Fawn x 0.1 Pied =
    Gray cocks and Pied (on head only: POH), split for fawn.
    Fawn hens (with or without POH), homozygous.

1.0 POH-pied-Fawn x 0.1 Fawn-POH-Pied =
    approximately half POH-Pied and Pied.
    Fawn-POH-Pied.
    Fawn-Pied in both sexes!

Hence: Fawn-pied x Fawn-pied =
    100% Fawn-pied.

1.0 Fawn-pied x 0.1 Pearled-pied =
    Pied cocks, split for Fawn and pearled.
    Fawn and pied hens, homozygous.

1.0 Pied, split for Fawn and Pearled x 0.1 Fawn-pied =
    Pied and Fawn-pied in both sexes.
    25% Pearl-pied hens, of which approximately half are Fawn-pearl-pied.

1.0 Pied, split for Fawn and Pearled x 0.1
    Fawn-pearled-pied =
    Pied, Fawn-pied and Fawn-pearl-pied in both sexes.

Hence: Fawn-pearl-pied x Fawn-pearl-pied =
    100% Fawn-pearl-pied.

Inos

Cock:

    Head and mask is present as with the gray Cockatiel; the back of the head and the neck are white. There should be a sharp demarcation between the yellow mask and the white back of the head. The same applies for the orange cheeks and yellow mask.
    Wings: white. Any markings are a defect.
    Yellow primaries are permissible.
    Body: white; yellow feathers around the legs (thighs) are allowed.
    Brown upper tail-coverts.

Central tail-feathers on top: white. Under tail-coverts, the secondary tail-feathers, and the underside of the tail-feathers are white-yellow.

Eyes: red.

Beak: horn-colored.

Feet: flesh-colored. Nails: horn-colored.

Hen:

Head and mask marked like the cock.

Wings: white with sometimes a yellow haze. The same applies for the primaries.

Body: breast, belly, thighs, and around the vent a deep, even yellow.

Tail: uppertail-coverts and top of the primaries vary from white to yellow.

Eyes: red.

Beak: horn-colored.

Feet: flesh-colored. Nails horn-colored.

This mutation is neither a lutino nor an albino. The color intensity depends on the gray Cockatiel used.

In the Ino-mutation the black eumelanin is almost totally pushed aside, so that the yellow color present becomes clearly visible.

The albino Cockatiel was one of the earliest color mutations and remains one of the most popular color varieties now being bred. *Photo by author*

A fawn hen (left) and a dilute male model their respective, highly-sought-after color mutations. *Wissink*

The albino is conclusively identified by the red eye, or visible blood supply in the organ of vision. In true albinos the eye shows a complete absence of its own pigment.   *Wissink*

It is interesting to note that even in the true albino form, the Cockatiel shows color in the crest, head and cheek patches. Albino Cockatiels also have some colored tail feathers.

Photo by author

131

A small, garden aviary will comfortably house one pair of adult Cockatiels. The birds will generally benefit from the outdoor environment and they will also enhance their own surroundings. *Photo by author*

A view of the author's own home aviaries. Each unit, or flight accommodates one color mutation. It the bird enthusiast can devote the space, this is the correct way to keep and breed Cockatiels.   *Photo by author*

The lutino is yet another popular color mutation of the little gray bird from Australia.
Wissink

This elegant pair are white Cockatiels with black eyes. They have pigment and so are not albinos. *Photo by author*

The amusing-looking harlequin shown here is known as a pied mutation.

Photo by author

7

Taming and Training

CONTRARY TO WHAT IS SO OFTEN SAID, there is no correlation at all between color and markings and temperament when looking for a Cockatiel to tame and train. Of course there are individual differences among tame Cockatiels. Some birds learn easier than others, but appearance has nothing to do with this. It is also untrue that only males can learn to talk; I have known hens, that possessed a vocabulary many male Cockatiels would be envious of. If you want to own a talking Cockatiel, look for a young bird, because they are more open to "suggestions" and will want to imitate the trainer without much ceremony. To achieve this, isolate the Cockatiel from his or her companions, and even from different species with which he may be housed in a large aviary. The young Cockatiel, especially a hand-fed youngster, makes the best pet. For he likes to be "cuddled" and enjoys the company of people. Sooner or later he may imitate the sounds of other birds. The fact that he does so may cause him to be inattentive to human speech and so retard training efforts. By not giving your Cockatiel the opportunity to catch sounds you don't want it to learn, the bird will give its attention to what you want to teach it and that's your initial objective.

Welcome Home

With the decision to purchase a young Cockatiel, two important questions arise, namely:

1. How do we transport a young, presumably untrained, Cockatiel to its new home?
2. How will we proceed to accustom the bird to its new surroundings?

137

Your new pet must never be collected from the bird dealer in an ornamental cage. These cages are generally far too big, and even if you were to wrap it in newspapers for the journey, the bird would flutter about in it wildly, risking injuries. In addition, once we get home, we will have an extremely tired and nervous young Cockatiel, that will be of no use for training for some time. For this reason we should transport our Cockatiel in a so-called traveling-cage; a box, usually made of stout cardboard or hardboard, with some ventilation holes punched in or with a piece of fine wire mesh. Of course it's possible to make such a cage yourself: the front side consists mainly of the wire mesh and the rest is made of wood. The dimensions are 12 x 10 x 10 inches. With a cardboard box, be sure the ventilation holes are not covered by labels, wrapping paper or similar material. On the bottom, throw sufficient seed; also—especially if you have a long journey to make—provide some moist bread, so your new Cockatiel will not have to endure thirst. Don't worry that the bird might not be able to find the seed in the dark; Cockatiels will search for seed in the near darkness of the transportation-cage; during a study-sojourn my wife and I regularly saw Budgerigars, Rosellas, Cockatoos, Cockatiels and other birds foraging during the evening and at night, even if there was little moonlight. Also with our aviary Cockatiels we were able to establish that the birds searched for food at night. From this all we may draw the conclusion that transporting Cockatiels over a longer distance is quite possible. As long as the birds are provided with seed (and possibly some moist bread), they can be transported by any means, car, airplane or train in the traveling-cages mentioned herein, providing that the time between departure and arrival does not exceed four hours.

On arriving home, first be positive that all doors and windows are closed, that there are no open fires, that our gas or electric oven is not turned on at the time, and fans have been turned off. If all that has been done, move the Cockatiel from his traveling-cage to his ornamental cage. The best way to do this is to leave the doors of both cages open opposite each other; usually the bird will calmly climb over, given enough time.

If possible, install the newcomer in his new abode before noon, so it will have all day to adjust to the new cage and surroundings; it will then also be able to find the various perches with ease and choose one as a permanent sleeping place. Cockatiels placed in new homes during the evening will flutter and scramble about restlessly all night, and the chance for injuries is very great.

Most newly purchased birds come from an aviary or a large flight, others will come from the well-known barred parrot-cages, and are therefore accustomed to seed cups and drinking fountains. Still, keep a sharp eye on the newcomer—from a distance—and be sure he finds the seed cup quickly. Most birds learn this at their place of birth, the bird seller's establishment, or in quarantine, but just to be sure the bird will eat well, scatter some seed on the bottom of the cage. A Cockatiel will instinctively search for food on the ground and therefore doesn't have to starve. Even though a full seed cup might be right above its beak, if the Cockatiel is not acquainted with similar utensils (for example hand-fed Cockatiels), it might take some time for him to figure out what their purpose is and what's in them. Also that a Cockatiel wants to eat "at ease" after a very tiring journey isn't hard to understand; and if he isn't able to find forage immediately, that won't be exactly beneficial to his "peace of mind." Once the Cockatiel has found his food, then this "tracking" will no longer (the seed can perferably be strewn in the direct proximity of the seed cup) be necessary.

First Steps Toward Successful Training

The first few days in a new home are the most stressful for a Cockatiel. Yet you must not give the bird to be trained too much rest; as if you start training immediately, you will have the best chances for success. As soon as the Cockatiel sits in his ornamental cage, carefully put your hand inside (for the time being inside a strong leather or canvas glove); the Cockatiel will accept your hand as being part of the "furniture" in the cage, especially if you move your hand slowly up and down. More than once a young Budgerigar or a young Cockatiel seated himself on my finger or hand within fifteen minutes after arrival in my home.

When you give the bird fresh drinking or bath water, when feeding it and whenever you are occupied with it, call it by name with a clear voice. Choose a short, easily repeated name like Bobby, Jackie, Polly, Peter or Johnny that the bird can imitate without extra speech training. If this is not successful, other ways, with which I will deal later on, will be tried.

As soon as the bird realizes that the hand put inside does not change anything in the cage, nor harms him in any way, it won't take it long to accept your hand as a normal "phenomenon" being part of the cage. One Cockatiel will accept your hand sooner than the other; in the latter case keep up your efforts. Don't lose patience under any circumstance, because any unexpected movement of your hand will be experienced as something new. Move your hand slowly and wait till the bird accepts it.

As soon as the Cockatiel perceives that the hand put inside the cage is not a threat, the hand will be examined and after it has been approved, will be accepted without much ado and also used as a "perch." Once the bird has progressed this far, put an index finger under the body very carefully, and press softly against the abdomen just above the legs; the bird will then usually seat itself on your outstretched finger without difficulties; if this does not succeed at first, continue the first exercise using the hand as the old familiar seat. If after a few days you see that the hand is once more accepted without fear, attempt the finger method again.

If necessary, move your index finger softly but "coercively" across the abdomen; usually the bird will step over onto the finger. If the bird should start to flutter wildly and show fright, you must under no circumstance

139

withdraw your hand, as it is very possible that the bird assumes—as far as an animal is capable—that it has "scared away" your hand, and therefore it is likely to repeat the action. Don't withdraw your hand from the cage before some success, however small it may be, has been achieved.

Outside the Cage

Once your Cockatiel is finger-tame teach it also to step back from your finger to the perch. To accomplish this, hold the Cockatiel resting on your finger with his breast against a perch; a command such as "up" can be useful. When he knows this perfectly, after several days take him out of the cage while he is on your finger. The first trip outside the cage must be short. Your Cockatiel will probably fly around the room and inspect things the first time he is out of his cage. After a few days you'll notice that the bird chooses a special spot, preferably close to mirrors, windows and other shiny objects, in which he can see himself. Remember any places (or place) of preference, so you'll know where to look for him, if he has left the cage. Actually, letting Cockatiels fly around the room freely is quite risky, considering that there may be fragile objects in the room, and apart from the fact that such a bird, having a considerable wingspan, might easily injure itself in the relatively small space, that most rooms actually are.

A well-trained Cockatiel will return to the cage immediately if the trainer so wishes; at first you can lure the bird back with a food reward; later these treats will not be offered. Again it is wise to use a fixed command, such as "come." If the bird refuses to "come," despite repeated commands, use a thin bamboo stick with a diameter of about ½ inch or a perch shaped like the capital T at least ½ inch in diameter to recover him.

The bird will usually climb onto the stick, especially if you press the stick softly against the abdomen. Slowly move back to the cage, while the bird sits on the stick. But it is still preferable to train your Cockatiel so well that he returns to his cage immediately after the command "come." If you have to go "bird-catching" all the time, not only will it be unpleasant and tiresome for the bird, but it will also leave you frustrated and unsatisfied.

Once your Cockatiel obediently returns to his cage whenever you want him to, proceed with the next stage—teaching him to go from one hand to the other. Let him jump or step from one hand to the other as much as he wants; this is a very relaxing occupation for you as well as for the bird. When the Cockatiel understands this too, it won't take long before he explores other parts of your body as well (arm, head, shoulder, etc.). Finally having reached this point, you can really say you have a hand-tame Cockatiel.

Training With a T-Perch

A T-shaped perch most resembles a natural resting place and can therefore be used best for training. Many bird-trainers prefer using their finger during the first training sessions (the method mentioned before), others prefer a T-shaped perch. Such a perch must never be too smooth, and if it is, it can be roughened with sandpaper; of course, you should take care that there are no splinters on it.

But before we go on, let's take note of this: perhaps you already know that birds cannot determine by appearance, whether they are dealing with males or females. It's the behaviour through which birds recognize gender; for example the characteristic aggressiveness of males when they look at each other. On the other hand, when a hen looks at the male, she will slant her head to one side, look away, and more or less neglect the male. If she is interested in the male, she will watch him closely while making nodding and bowing movements, the tail spread like a fan, and produce small clattering sounds with her beak. Now you will probably say that this may all be very interesting, but it doesn't have anything to do with the subject, the T-shaped perch!

Well yes, it does! Actually, it's a serious mistake to point a perch (or finger or hand) straight at a sitting bird and slowly approach it. This resembles an approaching, aggressive male Cockatiel. The only way to approach a bird with a T-perch is from the side and very, very slowly. As soon as the Cockatiel perceives the perch it is—if your timing is right—already too late and he will not want to perch on it, so now you make the bird sit on the perch by pressing it softly against the abdomen (at the height of the feet). If the bird spots the perch sooner than you mean it to, move the perch slowly away from its immediate reach and start again by bringing the perch towards the bird from the side. It is not necessary to start all over from the other corner of the room; you start right where you were standing when the bird perceived the T-perch. If it backs out again away from the perch, wait till the bird has calmed down again before making a new attempt. Stay right where you were in the last attempt.

The same procedure can be followed to get the bird out of the cage without using the finger method, but with the T-perch. Do not take the T-perch out of the cage until the Cockatiel has learned his lesson, so that he will accept it as being part of the furniture in the cage. Most cages have a detachable bottom, so it won't be a problem to lay the T-perch on the floor or place it inside against the bars via the bottom. Sometimes it appears with this method that the bird reacts better and easier when approached from behind; the perch is moved across the back and head under the abdomen in a semi-circle and subsequently the bird is "forced" onto the perch by light upward pressure. Again this upward pressure may be strong, so that at no reaction the bird is more or less slowly lifted from its seat. Pay attention if the bird begins nodding nervously and appears to be getting jumpy; in such a case it is wise to wait for a few minutes until the bird has calmed down again, or else the bird may start fluttering and scrambling about its cage restlessly, which will only make it more upset and perhaps afraid of the T-perch.

During the whole training period talk to your bird. It doesn't matter what

141

you say, as long as you say something! The human voice often calms the bird and inspires trust. And don't give up the lesson unless the bird makes some progress, no matter how small it may be. So, in the case mentioned above: go on till the bird has placed itself on the T-perch, and after some well-meant, encouraging words, back to its usual perch, by pressing the latter against the abdomen, right next to the feet. This can sometimes be very tiresome for the trainer and it may take some time, but giving up is out of the question; the bird should learn something in a session, even if it is only a little, otherwise the rest of the training will become a difficult and tiresome occupation that you won't enjoy very much, and neither will the Cockatiel.

The Ladder

When after many lessons the Cockatiel steps upon your finger, hand or T-perch without hesitation, you can teach him, outside the cage, to climb onto the index-finger of your other hand or on a second T-perch. Remember to talk to him and praise him if he reacts correctly. Personally I first let the bird step once or twice onto my finger (or hand) or to the second T-perch in this new lesson.

If the Cockatiel has performed it properly once or twice, put him back into the cage which he considers a "safe harbor."

After having learned something new—however simple that may seem to you—the bird will be enthusiastic, even though it may not be immediately apparent. Therefore, to calm it down, the right thing to do is to put it back in its cage for a little while. After half an hour repeat the process; now let the bird step back and forth four or five times. Perched on your finger, or T-perch it will probably look around the room inquisitively and even fly around a bit—no real harm in that of course. If the bird is well-trained it will return to your finger, T-perch or its cage when you want it to.

In any case it would be sensible not to have anything in the room that can distract its attention, for instance a radio playing, a record player or TV set. Once the bird is accustomed to stepping from finger or perch back into its cage, the moment has arrived to slowly walk our pupil, perched deftly on either hand, finger or perch, around the room, while talking reassuringly to it. If this has gone well put the bird back in its cage for half an hour and then try again. A bit of good advice: raise your extended finger, hand or perch a little above your own height if you can; a bird prefers to go to roost as high as possible; it makes it feel safe. A voice nearby may make it uneasy (for the time being anyway), although it's probably used to your voice by now.

Now start using the second T-perch, forefinger or the hand itself. Make the Cockatiel step from one perch to the other or from one forefinger to the other, in the familiar way, by light pressure on his abdomen; at the same time imitate a staircase by holding the right-hand perch a bit lower than the left-hand perch; the same applies for your fingers or hands. Now you can make the bird go up or down as you please as if it were climbing a ladder.

When you try this for the first time the young bird will usually start flying about. Calmly return it to its cage and try again after half an hour; you'll undoubtedly succeed in due course. Don't make your Cockatiel nervous; if it flutters to the ground, approach it slowly, hold out your forefinger and quietly wait and see if it will accept it; use the same procedure if with a T-perch or your hands. Speak to the bird and don't rush anything! If it flies or walks away, wait till it calms down and starts inquisitively taking in its surroundings; then approach it again, while speaking to it calmly and in a quiet voice. If it becomes necessary to catch the bird without delay, throw a towel, sweater or similar article over it. Try not to catch it with your hands, because a nervous Cockatiel will bite under all circumstances; and bite he can, believe me!

The best way to hold a Cockatiel in any case is to let the bird's back rest against the palm of your hand. The head is between your thumb and middle-finger; your forefinger over its head, as if it were a "helmet." Your ringfinger is level with its stomach, your little finger rests behind its legs or in line with its tail.

It will be clear that once the bird has learned to move from perch to perch, introducing a ladder will be easy enough. I found that I obtained best results by practicing these lessons in front of a large mirror; the bird sees itself, wants to imitate itself and in short, tries its very best to captivate its reflection; more than one bird was even so intent on acting up for its double in the mirror that it seriously fell in love with itself.

Nothing is wrong with that as long as you continue giving the bird your attention and leave it alone during its romantic spells.

As already stated, training should start as soon as possible when the birds are quite young, although older birds can also learn a lot with intensive work. Many trainers raise the young birds by hand once they are independent of parents.

When a young, hand-raised Cockatiel doesn't come into close contact with other birds it often sees its keeper as its real mother or father, and it will irrevocably accept him or her as a member of the same species, however unkind that may sound.

In their behavioral patterns many animals show a tendency to accept the first object they see as a parent and member of the species, especially when there are no other congeners or other animals around. Ducks, hatching from the egg, follow the first object that moves; if that happens to be a human they will follow it. Biology shows many examples of this tendency. Therefore, as you will probably have realized by now, training and taming Cockatiels (or other parrots) isn't difficult at all as long as you do it with patience and devotion. Because the keeper/aviculturist is seen as a father or a mother and because its behavioral pattern is formed for a large part by copying set examples and so on, certain games are very easy for a young Cockatiel to learn.

143

A Cockatiel should never be allowed to spend its entire life in solitary confinement in a cage without any special attention from its owner. Tame, trained Cockatiels and other parrots may be left together; if you have untamed birds, keep them away from the trained ones; if you have one trained bird, give it a lot of attention daily—I can't emphasize this enough—but best keep it away from other birds, because it sees its keeper as a friend and a member of the species. Personally I find it better to keep all trained birds separated. This isn't absolutely necessary however, as I have explained above. Of course you can let trained birds "perform" as a group, but as soon as the performance is over, separate them from one another again; in that way you can prevent the birds from taking over each other's tricks. There's nothing fundamentally wrong with that of course, but there is always a chance that the bird will stop paying attention to its keeper.

From what I have said on the subject so far, it may appear that hand-raised Cockatiels can only be trained with the utmost difficulty if they can be trained at all. I have also said, that is definitely not the case. In fact it isn't more difficult to do; it only requires a little more time, trouble and patience. If you are prepared to give your bird the attention it deserves regarding these three points you will certainly be able to turn even somewhat older birds into good pupils.

Tricks

In high school we probably heard that all animals learn through association. The Russian scientist Pavlov previously demonstrated this with dogs; everytime they were fed, a bell was sounded. After some time the dogs would start salivating even if the bell was rung without their being fed. In other words: Pavlov had taught the dogs to associate the sound of a bell with food. In view of our training this is an important detail to consider. Reward the bird for everything it does well. In no time it will associate a well-performed trick with a reward, for instance a bit of tasty (sensible) food. To put it another way: the bird will realize that the reward is a consequence of its action.

What kind of reward then?

You could try some millet. That's sensible and delicious for a Cockatiel. Birds often get bored when they are in training or during a "performance." It may seem as if they can't keep their minds on the subject at hand. The best way to revive their attention is to use a "cricket": the well-known toy that makes a snapping sound when the tongue is depressed. The birds immediately react to this sound and show a rekindled interest in the "game"; of course you should reward them for their behavior with a few tasty seeds.

No Food

A few hours before the first training session, remove the food-cups from

144

the cage. Once the bird is used to your hand you may hand-feed it. First try some millet or some other seed it likes and snap the "cricket" as soon as it accepts the food. Every time you give your bird something especially delicious make the same snapping sound and before long it will associate the sound with the food it likes so well.

What games and tricks can you now teach the bird? There are numerous possibilities of course and the bird itself will also discover and even design its own games and tricks. One of my Cockatiels, for example, clearly enjoyed taking a coin from my desk and letting it drop into an empty ashtray. Once the penny lay in the ashtray the bird would return for a second coin and repeat this till there were no coins left. Then he would transfer all the coins to the edge of the desk and drop them on the floor. When he had finished this task as well he would fly to the floor, take each coin into his beak and put them in the ashtray once again. If he was willing to repeat the whole procedure more than twice— to the delight of my little daughter—I would scatter some goodies (usually millet) in the ashtray and summon him with my cricket to take a well-deserved rest. If he tired of the game he would come and sit on my shoulder or head, pleased as punch!

Clipping Wings

Clipping a few flight feathers to prevent the bird from escaping before it is completely tame is a side of our hobby on which I don't hold a definite opinion. I have worked with birds that have had their wings clipped as well as with birds that did not and I really couldn't say which birds were the easier to work with.

If you treat the bird in a calm and controlled manner it will not make much difference, in my opinion; and of course the decision for or against may also depend on the temperament of the individual bird. Start training your bird without clipping its wings. If you find your pupil is rather obstinate, clipping a few flight feathers could be a good idea.

If you are for clipping, try doing it on one wing only, using a sharp pair of scissors. Clipping a bird's wing won't hurt it and after a while the clipped feathers will be replaced by new ones (during the molt). If the bird isn't fully trained yet when it starts growing new feathers, another clipping will be necessary, of course.

Children and Cockatiels

It's hard to say who gets the most fun out of a companionship: the Cockatiel or the child. From what I said earlier it has probably become clear that Cockatiels are very affectionate and always willing to play games. Because they are easily tamed and because they can quite literally imitate the human voice these birds are a constant delight.

On the practical side, pet Cockatiels can be an asset to a child's education.

Not only can they help teach children the wonders of Nature, but by letting children take care of the animals, we can also impart to them a love for the natural world in general, and respect for all living things. In these times filled with mindless violence, so insecure and without love, taking care of and caring for birds can give one a great deal of spiritual and physical satisfaction.

Often, observing the tame Cockatiel and the child will give the *adults* in the family the greatest pleasure.

Talking Cockatiels

As soon as the Cockatiel is tame to the hand you may start considering speech lessons. Not every Cockatiel however is a gifted pupil; nor is every parrot for that matter.

In any case, teaching a male or a female doesn't make the slightest difference. If the bird has been raised by hand, directly from the nest, as is true of nearly every young bird on the market, the learning of certain words and/or short sentences won't present any serious problems. Obviously, not every bird, raised from the nest, will become an excellent speaker. Teaching Cockatiels, even those a few years old, is possible as long as the training is done with patience and perseverance. But before you start speech lessons it is important for the bird to feel completely at ease with you. You must also see to it that the bird isn't frightened by children nearby, a radio playing or by any other distracting noise.

If the bird you're training to talk is frightened during the first few days, only kindness can win back its trust and secure its undivided attention for the things you wish to teach it. This won't happen in just a few days. It can sometimes even mean several weeks of hard work! New birds should therefore always be placed near people so they can observe what goes on around them.

Don't keep your birds too close to household activity either; no noises or anything else happening around the house should be allowed to frighten them or make them nervous. Remember that birds that are only given their daily food and drink and are further left to themselves will never grow tame and will certainly not learn to speak. Constant attention and kindness are needed to make the bird trust and love you. If you can't succeed in this with your Cockatiels it will be very difficult indeed to tame them and teach them to talk. One could hardly expect any results if that is the case.

Intelligence

A bird that talks or performs tricks only imitates; animals—including our Cockatiel—can't reason. They cannot "think" in the literal sense of the word; even though the opposite seems to be the case! The Cockatiel is taught to imitate and to repeat, or to do things which have attracted his attention and piqued his curiosity. The bird can only be taught to repeat certain sentences and to use the right answers at the most suitable moments. A bird is not taught

146

to say "Good night" at six o'clock in the morning or to say "Good bye" when someone pays a visit. The bird is taught to say certain words and/or sentences at the appropriate times of the day.

Male or Female

I firmly believe and have often repeated that it makes no difference with which sex one starts training. Both sexes are equally capable of learning to speak and to perform tricks. Often the trained birds are only the trainer's favorite pupils and nothing more; there is no way most trainers could tell the sex of the birds. This is different in the case of the breeder for whom sex of the birds is very important.

Only one conclusion is possible here: children and women make the best speech instructors. The pitch of children's and women's voices is easier for the Cockatiels to imitate than those of men and post-pubescent boys.

Covering the Cage

Covering the bird's cage with a cloth or a newspaper during our first lessons is a widely-accepted practice. I personally don't believe that this will bring a positive result; I have always thought that the bird likes to see *and* hear the trainer. But this statement is naturally based on personal experiences. If your bird learns better and faster when it is screened from the world outside, then you should certainly follow this plan in your training sessions. Covering the sides and the back of the cage appears to increase the bird's concentration in most cases, because distraction is limited to a minimum.

Demanding Your Bird's Attention

Demand your Cockatiel's attention during all training sessions and set the stage to give you best results. Providing solid toys, mirrors and similar objects is unwise at the commencement of training. The bird cannot fully concentrate on its lessons with these distractions present and your results will be disappointing.

Do not train more than one bird at the same time. Attempting to train two birds in the same room, even in different cages, is foolish as the birds will imitate each other and will not learn or be interested in what we want to teach them.

Abusive Language

Too many trainers, it seems, like to teach their birds to repeat offensive and obscene language. This is very childish and far from appropriate. Remember that profanity and insulting phrases may be used by the bird at times and in places which are not at all becoming. Teaching objectionable language is not difficult, in fact teaching these words is simplified because of

147

the often sharp and unusual combination of the sounds. Still, this is a poor excuse for teaching birds things they do not understand and which might offend many hearers, and adversely affect children.

A Sample Training Method

Many who teach psittacine birds to speak have arrived at the conclusion that the process takes less time than it originally appeared. Children, by comparison, do not learn to speak within a few months, and it often takes more than two years before our infants formulate anything understandable or sensible. Therefore, practice patience if you want to teach your Cockatiel to speak; patience and love.

Don't punish the bird if it appears uninterested, but treat it with love and affection. Experience has taught many trainers that the mornings are the best times for speech lessons, while Cockatiels can also be successfully trained between seven and nine o'clock in the evening.

The cage may, except for the front side, if desired, be screened and the trainer may place himself so that the bird can hear, but not see him or her. Then the bird's concentration proves greater than when the bird can see the trainer's every move.

The words or the short expressions must be uttered clearly in the same pitch and always at the same speed. Don't use any other expressions or other words during the lesson than those which the bird must learn to speak. After every 15 minutes, take a five-minute break to let the lesson sink in.

Make sure there are no distracting sounds during these breaks: it is sensible for the trainer not to speak with anyone within hearing distance of the Cockatiel nor that he sings or whistles a tune to a song on the radio at this time. After the break start again with the same expressions, words or whatever is being taught.

In the evenings, proceed in the same way. Don't praise the bird until it has mastered certain words or expressions faultlessly, so that certain sounds and impurities are not taken up with the word that should be learned.

Aside from specific speech-lessons, it can help to say the word or the expression regularly when we enter the room in which the bird is kept. The morning greeting also consists of the teaching material, just as your "good night" when you turn off the light at night to go to bed does.

If, after a reasonable time, all your attention and instruction does not work, you will have to try a different method. Train in a half-darkened room twice a day, in short sessions no longer than a half hour. Sit with the bird so it can hear you, but not see you. Eventually you will discover that the bird starts repeating the words it has learned. Never lose patience or punish the bird. Punishing always has the opposite effect, and the bird will have had enough of speech-lessons, not to mention its shattered confidence. You can, with a single gesture or word, turn a sweet and gentle animal into a nervous and aggressive creature which is no longer tractable.

Under all circumstances we must be aware of the fact that we are "working" with animals which only and always ask our greatest love and which, if it is given to them undividedly, will reward you with gratifying devotion and affection.

Using Bird Psychology in Training

If you want your Cockatiel to say simple phrases like "Good morning" or "Good bye," practice such expressions respectively only in the morning or in the latter case together with a partner who is leaving the room time and again. The association of time and deed (here, the spoken word) is remarkably strong with psittacines and other talking birds. Seldom will it say the expression, if taught with dedication and intelligence, in the evening or at night, or call out enthusiastically to someone entering the room. When a bird is taught to say the name of a certain seed or a certain type of food, practice this of course, when the bird is fed this food; very soon it will repeat the name of the food when it sees it. It is also striking that Cockatiels and other psittacines learn easily to pronounce the names of family members and use them properly!

Many fanciers think that taming and teaching the Cockatiel to speak can be done at the same time. Personally I think it is better first to tame the bird and then to teach it to speak. Nevertheless many trainers, who give their birds speech-lessons, tame them at the same time with very successful results.

The most usual method of taming the bird and teaching it to talk at the same time is as follows: remove food and water containers from the cage, as soon as the new bird arrives. Also remove food and water trays first thing in the afternoon and hope that the animal has been able to get enough food during transport. You can give the newly arrived Cockatiel a few hours to get used to cage and food, and only then remove food and water trays temporarily (a method I would prefer).

Early in the morning of the second day feed the new bird by hand all the sweet treats he is entitled to, while speaking the expressions or words the Cockatiel is to learn. Every time you teach the bird, offer it food and do this until the Cockatiel repeats your words faultlessly.

When the bird is ready for a second expression or a few other new words, use the same procedure. In the end food will no longer be the main motivation, but the trainer. The bird will happily learn other words when you are in the immediate area. Then the time comes to give the Cockatiel its daily food normally without feeding it by hand. Then only your presence is enough for your friend to perform its entire repertoire. Thanking the bird now and then with some sweet treats is, of course, advisable.

Now it often happens that the bird stops talking as soon as you come to its cage. The bird more or less uses what it has learned to "lure" you to its cage. Once you are there the bird will look at you with its shrewd eyes and still remain silent. If you are about to go away again it will undoubtedly surprise

149

you with a torrent of words and expressions, with the sole purpose of changing your mind and making you stay.

Further, it is unwise to stop the lessons after a few words or expressions have been taught, as the first few words are the most difficult to teach; but once the bird has taken to learning words, then teaching it new words or expressions is, quite often, child's play.

You will continually have to give the Cockatiel your full attention, and you will have to continue in the usual concentrated way, and if a rehearsal appears to be necessary, you must not refrain from it. You can not get a good talking Cockatiel with little effort.

Tape Recorders

I've heard several records with detailed instructions on how to train parrots, parakeets and Mynah birds, and how to teach them to speak. If you want your bird to learn to speak quickly, a record like that can be very handy, especially if you have little or no time to train the animal yourself.

An excellent record is undoubtedly *Train Your Bird in Stereo* by the famous American aviculturists Henry J. Bates and Robert L. Busenbark. There is a clear and interesting instruction booklet with the record. The best way to obtain information about this is to write to Audubon Publishing Company, 3449 North Western Avenue, Chicago, IL 60618.

It is cheaper, of course, if you have a tape recorder at your disposal, with which you can have enormous success as you can for example record the first expression or the first words you would like the bird to repeat. The only expense is one extra tape on which you record the lesson required. Later you can play this tape as often as you like or better still until the Cockatiel can repeat certain things faultlessly. While the bird listens and, as we hope, also tries to repeat what he hears, you can leave the bird on its own and do what you like, for a Cockatiel not only imitates the words, but also the intonation and the pitch, and it will therefore be fully concentrating, not realizing whether you are present or not.

Sooner or later your Cockatiel will appear not to limit itself to words or short expressions, but with just as great an effort it will try to imitate the whistling of other birds or the bark of your dog. I have known parrots that could faultlessly imitate the creaking sound of a wheelbarrow, the squeak of a badly oiled door and grandfather's smoker's cough!

A sound runs a good chance of being picked up by the bird as long as the sound which could be imitated catches the bird's attention long enough and often enough.

You have been warned, so take care.

For those who worry about the well-being of their pets, teaching psittacines or Mynah birds to talk or training them to do all sorts of tricks need not involve any cruelty to them. In the odd 25 years I have worked with birds (and many other species of other animals) both as a hobby and in my
150

work as a biologist, I have observed that both the bird and the trainer are having a pleasant time together.

Cockatiels and Technology

Parrots can learn more than 100 words, whole songs and phrases and even sentences which have to be spoken at the right moment. Most parrots can bear with difficulty, however, when a radio, television set or phonograph is playing and they will disregard all words and/or expressions and react naturally by screaming as long and loudly as possible. Then they will compete at screaming loudest. Parakeets, too, are inclined to do this, and a couple of Budgies or a few Cockatiels will persist in trying to scream louder than my wife's piano playing.

However, most birds seem to be very sensitive to soft, tuneful music for I have often observed parrots, parakeets or Cockatiels softly swaying their heads to the rhythm of my wife's music.

If your Cockatiels continue screaming when a radio or television set is on, then it is best to cover the cage with a thick cloth and the screaming will soon stop.

However keep in mind that Cockatiels do not usually pick up a large selection of words and expressions (in comparison with many other psittacines), but they are quite capable of whistling tunes.

8

Keeping Your Cockatiel Healthy

Everyone understands the general meaning of health, but it is not easy to define the state precisely. Dictionaries give varying definitions: a soundness of body or a normal condition of body with all parts functioning well, whilst one authority merely states that it is an absence of disease.

The diagnosis of disease in all live animals, but especially in birds, is particularly difficult compared with man. A sick person is able to describe his symptoms to the doctor, but the veterinarian relies entirely upon his powers of observation and those of the patient's owner.

L. Arnall & I. F. Keyer in
Bird Diseases
An Introduction to the Study of
Birds in Health and Disease
(Copyright © 1975, TFH Publications, Inc.)

COCKATIELS PROVIDED with correct nourishment and housing, free from fumes, vermin and drafts, will generally maintain vigorous health. Of course unforeseen circumstances may occur that cause the birds to become ill and in need of our immediate help. One of the characteristics by which we can tell that a bird is not completely healthy is the drab color of its feathers: they are dull and lifeless.

Usually a sick bird looks that way. It appears apathetic and sits with ruffled feathers and often with its head drawn in between the feathers of its back. The bird often drags one of its legs and closes one or both eyes. Furthermore, if the bird's eyes are dull, this is a certain sign that something is wrong. Also, droppings of a sick bird are usually rather watery and are of an abnormal color.

A healthy Cockatiel sleeps with its head withdrawn between the shoulder feathers; however, if the pet is ill—it sits pitifully on the floor in a corner of the aviary, often with ruffled feathers—its head slowly dropping onto its chest.

In avian anatomy the last part of the intestine bulges slightly and empties into a cavity known as the *cloaca*. This cloaca is the only "exit" of the body for all wastes and for sperm and eggs as well. Since the urine mixes with solid waste, it is clear that the feces never really look hard and dry, but on the other hand the feces of a healthy bird are neither thin nor watery.

A bird's digestive tract differs from that of man. The bird must eat almost constantly. A Cockatiel can starve if it has to do without food for more than 30-35 hours or sometimes up to 48 hours, and this is of course just as valid for sick birds. Therefore never withhold food from sick birds (unfortunately this occurs all too often); try to make the pet eat and perferably its favorite food. Many sick birds did not die of their illness, but of hunger!

Handfeeding a Sick Bird

If a (usually young) bird refuses to eat, you shall have to feed it by hand (teaspoon or feeding syringe); several brands of specialized food are available and give complete satisfaction.

Boil 1 cup of milk and dissolve a few spoons of pancake syrup in it while it is still warm. Beat an egg yolk, add a pinch of salt and stir into the milk. If desired 100 milligrams of antibiotics may be dissolved in the mixture (ask your pharmacist for terramycin or aureomycin). This mixture can be refrigerated, but should be heated to 80° F for feeding.

Feed the mixture drop by drop.

To feed a sick bird or otherwise handle it, wrap the patient in a towel. In this way it cannot harm your hands or eyes or perhaps injure or exhaust itself as a result of unexpected movements.

Place the tip of the dropper (or teaspoon) in the corner of the beak and give two or three drops of nourishment at a time.

Be careful to never really squirt with the dropper, for you can easily cause the food material to penetrate the lungs, which, of course, is potentially disastrous.

Wait after each two or three drops until the bird has swallowed it all. Birds the size of large parakeets can take 14 drops per four hours, the smaller ones comparatively less and parrots a little more.

If the bird also suffers from diarrhea, give it a few drops of Kaopectate or some light biscuit with milk, or follow the instructions indicated under the

153

subject *Diarrhea*. Your bird dealer will undoubtedly also have many reliable remedies. Be careful, however, never to administer them simultaneously with the first-mentioned formula.

Leg Fractures

Bearing in mind how birds often behave in an aviary it is astonishing how relatively few fractures occur. Most fractures will also heal spontaneously, without much help from us. In dealing with large birds, such as parrots, it is usually necessary to set and splint the fracture. A bird with a leg fracture should be placed in a not-too-large cage without perches. Food and drink is offered in shallow, flat dishes on the floor. The point is that the patient, especially in the first few days, moves or exerts itself as little as possible. This also means that the cage should be placed in a quiet spot, away from playing children or curious, sniffing dogs or other pets and people.

In case of a wing-fractured Cockatiel, there is little or nothing you can do to help; however, when dealing with a strongly drooping wing, you can "stick" the wings in normal rest position with adhesive bandage or strong adhesive tape (such as freezer tape). For larger birds however, a cross bandage can be applied from under the belly between the legs.

It is understandable that thigh and lower leg fractures are extremely difficult to treat, especially if no professional help is available; the best we can do is to consult a veterinarian. The same applies to toe fractures which are difficult to treat and, in most cases, amputation is the only possible solution.

This leaves the portion of the leg between the ankle or hock joint and the foot, the so-called metatarsus, familiarly known to most lay persons as the "leg." Small birds, like Cockatiels and Budgerigars, can be helped with a chicken quill or a heavy drinking straw. Real straw will do nicely too! Halve the splint lengthwise and, after setting the fracture, apply the halves around it. Then wrap the length of the splint with woollen yarn, raffia or adhesive tape, but certainly not so tight as to prevent ligating.

Afterward, dress the whole in plaster and allow it to dry well. After about six to eight weeks you can remove the splint. Using acetone it takes but an instant, but take care not to drug the patient, and be sure to feed the patient plenty of fruit, vitamin D and some cod liver oil during the period it is wearing its "splint."

Diarrhea

Diarrhea occurs mainly as a result of neglect or malnutrition. At first it can be rather harmless, but when it continues over a longer period it can become quite dangerous, even deadly.

Nervous birds, when being handled, occasionally excrete thin droppings, but this situation returns to normal as soon as the animals are left to themselves again.

154

In this connection it is necessary to pay considerable attention to aviary cohabitants; if big, aggressive birds are placed in the same aviary with our smaller Cockatiels, it is easy to imagine that the latter will live under considerable stress.

Other forms of diarrhea are usually caused by some form of enteritis. There exist many causes: wrong or contaminated food, a cold caught because the patient was exposed to too many and too sudden changes of temperature, bacteriological infections are some examples. Only our immediate aid can save them; that is why it is comforting to know that various reliable medications are on the market. In addition to medicines, warmth is very important; maintain a constant temperature of 86-94°F (30-35°C). My experience is that warmth alone is often sufficient to cure a sick bird.

I also get extremely good results with infrared radiation treatment. We will irradiate one side of the cage, so that the sick bird will have the choice of sitting in the radiation or not. In other words: about half the cage should be out of reach of the radiation. A reliable heating device (a so-called "dark radiation emitter") is recommended because the bird must also have warmth at night. A small (15 watt) bulb burning will enhance the environment so that the bird can eat and (above all) drink if it wants to. Give the sick bird weak tea (without milk) or peppermint tea; I have obtained very satisfying results with the latter. Mix some pulverized charcoal through its favorite food and seed, and administer some tetracyclin, terramycin or aureomycin, as well as preparations containing vitamins and trace elements. If it appears to be an obstinate diarrhea consult a veterinarian without further delay. He will have recourse to stronger sulfonamides and antibiotics with which to treat the condition.

Note that diarrhea is not a disease but a clinical sign, a symptom; it accompanies a great many diseases and therefore should not be treated without first obtaining a correct diagnosis.

Nail Trimming

If aviary birds have the opportunity to climb sufficiently and wear away their nails on rough stones (flagstones are indispensable in aviaries) instances of overgrown nails will rarely, if ever, occur.

Of course, Cockatiels in cages are much more liable to have "trouble" with long nails than birds kept in aviaries. Use a sharp, strong pair of nail scissors, but be sure to do the job quite accurately, since you must avoid cutting the blood vessels which, by the way, are easily distinguishable if the nail is held against the light: the dark lines of the vessels then contrast with the horn of the nail.

If, however, a blood vessel is accidentally cut, a cotton pad dipped in styptic can help: press it against the blood vessel for a few minutes until the bleeding stops. A cotton pad with (non-caustic) iodine will also do.

It is very important to prevent the nails from growing too long. Besides

155

placing a few rough stones on the floor of the aviary, you can plant reeds in a corner, offer perches of several thicknesses and bark-covered breeding-boxes. Small covers are available on the market that can be fitted over perches; these covers are made of abrasive paper or sandpaper. It may help to provide cage birds with a floor *partially* covered with sandpaper. Avoid sharp tips and hooks on the clipped nails which might easily catch in almost any surface.

Iodized Salt

Mix some iodine-based salt through the seed once a week; this avoids enlargement of the thyroid gland (goiter).

Egg Binding

When nesting-places, space, diet and other breeding conditions do not conform to the conditions discussed in this book, it is certain that during breeding-season (or out of it!) some hens will have difficulty laying eggs.

If a hen is too fat, if it is exposed to drafts and cold during the time it is expecting eggs, or if the bird is too young, then the direct result will usually be egg binding.

Absence of/or insufficient egg-shells can also be caused by a lack of minerals, so that it becomes difficult to lay eggs (wind-eggs); in abnormal cases it could even lead to a rupture of the oviduct.

For this reason we should only use birds in perfect health and of the right age for breeding. The cloaca of a young hen is usually not sufficiently developed, which could lead to complications. Small species like Cockatiels, Budgerigars and Love birds should be at least 14-24 months old before breeding.

Sudden changes in temperature can also provoke egg binding.

Do not let the birds breed too intensively—under no circumstances permit more than three clutches a year. After the last round the parents need at least six months rest.

The symptoms of egg binding are easy to discern. The hen has ruffled feathers, usually sits on the ground (often in a corner on the aviary floor), frequently its eyes are partially or completely closed, its vent swollen and red; and often the patient will breathe heavily.

Pick up the bird carefully and place it in a separate cage without perches, maintaining a temperature of approximately 94° Fahr. A small quantity of olive oil, introduced in the anus by means of a small brush may lead to surprisingly good results. Half a teaspoon of glycerine, dissolved in the drinking water (with such a temperature even parrots and parakeets will drink) can bring relief. Because of the warmth the bird will regain command over its muscles and will usually lay its egg within the next few hours. If this does not happen apply some more olive oil to the cloaca; you could also hold the bird over a pan of steaming hot water; but the latter only if the hen does not deliver the egg after one or two efforts.

156

Avoid as much as possible taking the bird in your hands to prevent the egg from breaking in the body. Such accidents often lead to death by infection. If all this is to no avail, a veterinarian can break the egg out of the cloaca with forceps.

A rule of thumb to always keep in mind is to breed only Cockatiels of the right age in an aviary with a constant temperature. Do not forget to mix minerals, vitamins and some drops of cod liver oil through the favorite food before and naturally also during the breeding season. However be careful with mixing cod liver oil through the seed: never more than one or two drops per pound.

Pneumonia

Pneumonia is usually the result of a severe cold. The patient breathes agitatedly and heavily and a yellowish slime comes from its nostrils. The veterinarian cannot do anything more than give an injection with antibiotics in the breast muscles (intra-muscular) and hope for the best. Keep the bird warm and give it strong tea.

Eye Diseases

Cockatiels can easily contract an eye infection when they are exposed to drafts, have insufficient food or have been injured in a fight or a mating encounter. Some Cockatiels are very susceptible to eye diseases—particularly albino mutations.

We often treat these diseases with eye ointment or eye drops but, unfortunately, without a great deal of success. Actually, I have no objection to remedies, such as aureomycin and chloramphenicol eye ointment or neocortef eye drops, being used. However, sufficient antibiotics should be administered at the same time, either through an injection, for which the vet should be consulted, or through crop or beak. In which case tetracycline would be the best choice. Vibramycin, an antibiotic in the past often taken internally by children, may also be used. It has a great number of advantages. Little harm is caused if the quantity given is too great; it may be administered for weeks on end; it can be used as an antibiotic (known as doxycycline) against a wide variety of bacteria, and it needs to be taken only once daily to be effective over a period of 24-36 hours. As to dosage a safe rule of thumb is to administer 1½ to two drops per pound of body weight for about five days. Admittedly, though, Cockatiels recovered very quickly when five to six drops were given over a period of six consecutive days.

Eye infections always need to be treated with very great care, as pox, ornithosis, mycoplasm and a lack of vitamin A can also affect the eyes (eyelids—blepharitis). The eyes themselves may become infected, as often happens in the case of a cold (cataract), and total blindness can follow if action is not taken quickly.

157

As soon as you realize that a bird is suffering from an eye disease, the only sound advice to follow is: treat it as indicated above, disinfect the bird cage or aviary and consult a vet. Always be on the safe side. Do not take risks.

Goiter

Goiter or enlargement of the thyroid gland is particularly common among Cockatiels, Grass parakeets and Budgerigars.

Fortunately, this disorder no longer occurs very frequently, because cage sand available from pet shops is often treated with iodine. It is still widely found, however, in those areas where drinking water is deficient in iodine.

Goiter is not usually recognized by an external swelling. The growth, pressing against crop and windpipe, is internal. Clearly, any exertion, such as flying and running, will make the affected bird breathless very quickly. Breathing heavily it will drop to the ground, often with wide-spread wings and pendulous crop and neck. It may also make a high-pitched squeak or wheezing sound with each breath. In order to breathe more easily the bird will often rest its beak against the bars of the cage or on a parallel perch or tree branch. If you fail to act immediately, the disease will soon become worse. The bird may start to walk in circles and to suffer from infection to the head. Sudden death may then follow due to suffocation, heart failure or weakness through an insufficient intake of food.

In case of a serious endocrinal disorder the bird may be given iodine-glycerine—the proper mixture is one part iodine to four parts glycerine. Alternatively, a mixture consisting of nine parts parrafin oil to one part iodine-glycerine, administered with a nasal dropper in a corner of the beak intermittently over a period of three days, will work wonders.

It is, as you can see, possible for the owner, therefore, to play a healing role without too many problems and without having to call in a vet.

Feathers

To maintain the bird's relatively high body temperature of about 106° Fahr. feathers are of vital necessity. To be more precise, the inner covering or down feathers retain the air which has been warmed by body heat. Over these the outer covering feathers achieve more or less the opposite effect—preventing cold air from reaching the body beneath the feathers.

This is why most surface feathers are usually covered in a thin film of oil, and may also have a thin layer of powder, as happens in some species, such as Cockatoos. This powder or oil film also serves to prevent the skin beneath the feathers from becoming wet, leading to a harmful lowering of body temperature.

You may already know that young birds, whether they are still nestlings or have already left the nest, possess a lower body temperature than adult birds. They need, therefore, some warmth during the night and on cold days, and, if the young birds have left the nest, they should not be unnecessarily exposed to cold, wind or drafts. This is also why you should never disturb a nest, as this might cause the young birds to leave the parental home.

There is another reason why feathers are important although it is not so evident in Cockatiels (and other psittacines) as in peacocks, ducks, birds of paradise, weaver birds and Whydas. It is that birds often use their feathers as a means of courtship display. In short, feathers fulfill an important function just before and during the mating and breeding season.

Finally, feathers can be used either as a means of aggression or as a means of intimidation. By fluffing out its feathers a bird can enlarge itself and in this way frighten off a would-be attacker.

The most important function of feathers is, of course, to enable the bird to fly, although there are some species which have lost the use of their wings as implements of flight. The Ostrich and the various penguin species are probably the most widely-known examples.

There are three kinds of feathers:
1. contour feathers or pennae;
2. inner down feathers or plumulae;
3. filoplume feathers which grow together in small bundles.

Let us have a quick look at these types of feathers:
1. The contour feathers, as the name implies, give the bird its shape and provide insulation. They cover the bird's body entirely. Each species is usually marked by a somewhat constant number of these pennae at precisely the same places on the body as well as on the wings and tail. The chief feature of these feathers is that they have a rather long shaft;
2. The plumulae provide an extra insulation coat and have little or no shaft. They are found particularly on nestlings and between the contour feathers of adult birds;
3. Filoplume feathers appear to be degenerate feathers which look like hairs. They consist of a thin shaft or several thin shafts ending in a fine plume.

Bald Spots

When Cockatiels reveal *bald spots* outside of the molting period, parasites are the cause. The birds will also do a great deal of scratching. These parasites, such as bird lice and mites, must be forcefully dealth with. Bird lice usually hide by day in corners and crevices (often in nesting boxes and under perches), but come onto the birds at night to suck their blood. Mosquitoes and other damaging insects can cause a great deal of discomfort to our Cockatiels, particularly during the breeding season. Thanks to various sprays, you should be able to effectively rid your Cockatiels of any kind of parasite. Under no circumstances should you use DDT or lindane since these are extremely dangerous to the birds! Besides, their use is currently illegal.

159

Too great a difference in temperature can also cause bald spots on our Cockatiels. Quite often we have seen outside aviaries that are partially or even completely enclosed in glass; the temperature can rise so high during the day in such an aviary that it is more like a hot house than a house for birds. The nights, on the other hand, particularly in the spring, are often cold, so the temperature difference is really very great. This can easily cause the birds to develop bald spots, particularly on the back and head. Therefore, avoid these huge differences in temperature. This can be achieved by keeping the aviary open during the day instead of creating a greenhouse, which would be more suitable for tropical plants than Cockatiels.

Baldness can also be seen during the molting period. Providing the bald spots do not become too large, they are not a cause for concern. Molting birds need a great variety of food rich in vitamins and calcium. Experience has also taught us that birds should be housed in a spacious flight allowing for ample exercise. Exercise during the molt is a very important factor which should not be neglected. A lot of activity favorably influences the growth of the new feathers.

Cockatiels have their first molt at five to six months old, and thereafter, will molt once a year, usually during August and September.

Feather Plucking

An annoying habit is *feather plucking;* it can be the result of a vitamin deficiency, listlessness, boredom or overcrowding. It can occur in Cockatiels as it does in other species. Here again it is very important that their feeding program is carefully checked and improved if necessary. A disinfectant can be added to the drinking water temporarily. Fanciers who do not use city water but well water should add a trusted disinfectant to the water every day.

Listlessness and boredom can be alleviated by hanging up a few bunches of spray millet or weed seeds. Other suggestions are: sisal rope, which the birds will enjoy climbing very much, and pieces of raw red meat which will also keep them busy for a while. Beware of overpopulation. As soon as any birds start this nasty habit of feather plucking, they must be immediately put into a roomy cage by themselves.

Once the habit has become strongly ingrained, it is difficult to stop the birds. When they have completely given it up they may be put back with the other birds. Obviously all feathers should be promptly removed from the aviary or cage, otherwise the birds will start picking at the base of the quill, which contains a vitamin-rich marrow. If this is allowed the birds will never stop the habit.

Egg Pecking

A lack of calcium often turns some Cockatiels into egg peckers! In an otherwise smoothly functioning breeding operation, Cockatiels that start this habit will, of course, need to be "cured."

Boredom can also cause this irritating habit. Apart from cuttlebone and vitamins A and D, also offer your birds low salt grit and finely milled egg shell. If boredom is the cause, follow the same suggestions made under *Feather Plucking.*

Mineral Deficiency

Lack of essential minerals, especially calcium, can result in rickets—particularly in young birds. Those affected will have soft, bent legs on which they can hardly stand. Make sure they have sufficient intake of vitamins B and D to prevent this problem from developing.

Common Cold

The common cold is, I think, the illness that most frequently affects aviary birds. Most aviaries are not at all well protected from wind and drafts, and most fanciers start the breeding season much too early in the year. Temperature differences are another cause of the birds catching cold. It is absolutely essential, especially for imported birds (which are still entering the country, in spite of the Australian ban on their export) to get used to our cooler temperatures very gradually. This also applies to birds from Japan, which do not usually have strong constitutions. All this has made me an advocate of aviaries divided into three sections: a closed shelter, a covered flight and a completely open run. Thus the birds can sit and spend the night wherever they prefer. If they are acclimated gradually by staying in outer aviaries whenever weather permits, the result will be strong animals not susceptible to colds at the slightest breeze.

The moment you first notice something wrong with a Cockatiel, isolate him in a warm place. Heat is the first step toward recovery. Experience has shown that it is often sufficient to isolate the bird in a separate room, especially if some extra warmth is provided. Obviously, a sick bird should not be placed near or under a window or door that is regularly opened; no draft is allowed, not even during airing.

Special cages are available for sick birds, looking rather like small glass show cases and heated from below with lamps. Opinions vary as to the correct temperature for such cages, but I personally have always had good results with the patients in an atmosphere of around 94.5° Fahr. This temperature must be reached gradually. Never put sick birds immediately adjacent to a heat source. Birds' bones are hollow, and filled with air. Sudden increased heat makes this air expand inside the bones, not only causing much discomfort and pain, but raising the real risk of death.

A patient suffering from a cold is also very well served with an ordinary box-type cage, one side of which receives no heat at all, while the other side is heated with an incubator lamp (the infrared radiator discussed in the section

161

on *Diarrhea*). An evenly distributed temperature can be achieved by putting the lamp at the correct distance from the bars, but try this out first without a bird inside. With this arrangement a bird can go to the dark, unheated part of the cage whenever it feels it needs no warmth.

Personally I think this is the best method; the bird will not become uneasy during convalescence from being forced to remain in the heat of the special sick or hospital cage. The observant owner will know that a bird is recovering when he sees it spend most of its time in the cooler part of the cage. Of course the heat treatment must initially continue day and night until the bird's appearance and behavior indicate that it is well again. The smoothness of the coat of feathers is the best indicator of the patient's health. In addition to heat as a curative, drugs like sulfonamides and antibiotics can be used and are available from many good pet stores.

If a bird suffering from a cold makes sniffling noises and if a slimy fluid issues from its nostrils, while it is also suffering from diarrhea, the cause is probably germs (cocci, salmonella, etc.). Immediately consult a vet in such a case, especially if expensive mutations and/or parakeet varieties are involved. The doctor will prescribe antibiotics or sulfonamides, and advise you to keep the bird in a warm place.

Obesity

Birds that suffer from lack of exercise (because their cage is too small or because their owner has not provided anything to keep them occupied, so that they get bored), as well as those that do not get the right nutrition, are most liable to fall victims to obesity. Getting fat is however a very slow process. The owner must watch very carefully to spot the first signs. When the birds can barely sit on their perches anymore, things have already gone too far. The birds sit on the bottom of their cage, panting heavily, and do not seem to want to move. The contours of their bodies have become blurred, heavy and cylindrical and the skin appears yellowish when the feathers are blown apart: the fat shining through the skin! Just blow on the breast or abdominal feathers of such a bird and you will know what I mean.

Cockatiels suffering from obesity live much shorter lives than those that have plenty of exercise and lively interests. The sick ones have difficulty molting and just sit looking thoroughly bored.

The first thing is to give the birds plenty of exercise: hang some strong sisal ropes in the aviary and a few bunches of spray millet or weed seeds; they will love playing with those.

Then improve their nutrition, strictly by the book if need be, and provide lots of well-washed greens of fruit free from chemicals, but definitely no food with a high protein or fat content.

With any luck the "obese" bird will soon be his former self again, flying about as sprightly as before. Cage birds must be released in a secure area every day. Here they are allowed to fly freely for at least one hour. Birds receiving such daily exercise will not suffer from gout. Inside their cages your birds must get even more exercise. Put them in larger cages, or place perches farther apart, so that the bird is forced to make a greater effort to get to the other side. Do not work from the assumption: *My Cockatiel is fat, so if I don't feed it for a few days it will be all right again.* The bird must be fed, but with the right kind of food, for it will perish, however fat it may be, if it receives no nourishment.

Feeding Instinct

When Cockatiels display their feeding instinct, this is a sure sign of adulthood and of the urge to start breeding.

A male will try to win the affections of a female by offering her food, as if to show that not only now, but also later, when she is brooding or has a nest full of young, he is prepared to look after them and feed them. Lonely males of parrot species, especially Budgerigars, may be observed smearing reflecting objects in their cages (mirrors, glassware, porcelain) with partly digested food: they have fallen in love with their own images!

Such slimy seed cakes are seldom eaten again by the male bird. The owner often thinks there is something wrong with the animal, but this is not the case. The phenomenon can be explained quite naturally from the desire to start a family. The urge to regurgitate food, which is rather messy in the case of typical cage birds, can be tempered to a certain degree with the German product "Anti-Trieb," which is available from most good pet stores.

Warmth

Although most Cockatiels are kept in garden aviaries, they cannot remain outdoors during the winter months without our taking certain protective measures. Not only is it necessary for each aviary to have a shelter protected from wind, rain, and drafts, but its open end must also face south. If this should be impossible, it must be as much to the south as possible, south-easterly rather than south-westerly. The aviary can be "dressed up" on the outside with suitable plants so that it harmonizes with its environment and is not felt to be an eyesore in the garden.

Although most psittacines can endure temperatures down to about 48° Fahr. quite easily, the majority prefer a little more warmth: about 61-76° Fahr. Therefore, when it is necessary to move the birds to their night shelter or, failing that, to a place in the attic away from frost, if necessary use an infrared radiator as an extra heat source. Frost is always dangerous; birds inclined to spend the night outside in the run may suffer from frozen toes, especially those that rest so high on their legs that the toes are not protected by a warm "blanket" of abdominal feathers. Of course we must acclimate all our birds gradually by often forcing them to roost outside in spring and summer

163

whenever weather permits. Once the birds are accustomed to our climate and to their accommodations they will develop extremely sturdy constitutions and will seldom fall ill. Only when sudden unfavorable weather or temperature changes are expected (every bird lover keeps an eye on the weather forecast) do you have to take precautionary measures to protect your birds.

Worms

The problem of worms is a growing one with which practically every bird keeper is confronted sooner or later. The two culprits are *Ascaridia* and *Capillaria. Ascaridia* are fibre-thin worms, about 4 to 5 cm long, which live in the upper part of the intestinal tract. *Ascaridia maphrodita,* which are found in the parrot family, are probably prevalent all over the world. They will be mainly found in those birds which feed on the ground, wild birds not excepted. Budgerigars, Cockatiels, Love birds, Conures, Asiatic species like Ringneck parakeets, and many Australian parrots and parakeets are among the aviary birds found infected with these worms.

Capillaria are extremely thin and transparent, so that it is practically impossible to detect them with the naked eye in the bowel contents. These tiny worms also live in the intestines, surrounded by the catarrhal slime engendered by their irritating effect on the intestinal wall. With a little of this slime prepared on a glass plate we can observe the *Capillaria* worms under the microscope. They have the approximate thickness and length of a mouse hair.

According to Mr. R. van Damme of Zele, Belgium, from whom the author gained extremely useful information for this entry, both *Ascaridia* and *Capillaria* are true parasites: only the eggs can survive outside the host body. Worms driven out with an anti-worm treatment die quickly and are no longer infectious.

Parasitic worms have developed into extremely efficient egg-production machines. Tests have shown that an *Ascaridia* worm can lay between 2000 and 3000 eggs a day, in other words: one million eggs a year. Since an infected bird usually contains several worms it will be obvious that there may be millions of eggs on an aviary floor. *Capillaria* do not produce so many eggs.

The worms' eggs leave the bird together with the droppings. Newly excreted eggs must ripen first; they are not infectious until a number of days later.

The most dangerous period is during humid and warm weather, when the process takes about ten days. During cold weather it continues very slowly or stops altogether. Nevertheless the eggs retain their viability.

As soon as it gets warmer the eggs will ripen. Most eggs are ingested by the birds together with pieces of soil, hardly ever with food. Once inside the body the eggs will develop and the worm will attach itself to the inner wall of the bird's intestines. The larva will live for about a week, after which it dies and

164

becomes part of the bowel contents. The *Capillaria* will remain more or less in the same spot, the larva is fully grown after about six weeks, when it can in turn lay eggs.

The environment will be contaminated when an infected bird deposits its droppings. In certain weather conditions the eggs may be carried through the air to other places, so that the contagion spreads.

Luckily, worms' eggs are rather fragile, but they are very resistant to cold and moisture. Dry weather and intense sunlight kills them off. Eggs exposed to direct sunlight will die in a few days, but only in hot and dry weather. In other weather conditions they can survive with remarkable tenacity, even for a year or more!

Worms' eggs are very light and small; they may end up anywhere. They may float from one aviary to another and when a person steps in infected soil he is liable to infect any other aviary he enters.

Worms often cause the death of the bird they inhabit when they pierce the intestine wall (hemorrhagic enteritis). In any case, an infected bird is always weakened.

Since the worms are constantly surrounded by partly digested food, they can consume the best of the available proteins, vitamins and minerals. The intestines expand due to the proliferating worms. A cluster of worms can block the intestinal passage and in the final phase the bird dies from shock.

To ascertain the cause of a bird's death, we can have the veterinarian perform an autopsy. *Ascaridia* are easily discernible, but *Capillaria* can only be seen under a microscope. The bird must be cut open so that the intestines come out, after which the excrement can be pressed from the intestines with a knife, spatula, or other flat object.

If the infection is serious, the swelling of the intestine indicates that it is filled with worms, that have blocked the intestinal canal completely.

Usually, the many worms are not very big. However sometimes real "giants" may be found among them and when observing these specimens, even a layman won't question the harmfulness of these pests.

How can the bird keeper prevent infection from intestinal parasites?

Every bird has a certain resistance against parasites. If this were not so, all our aviary birds would be doomed.

Only when a bird is in poor condition, or suffers from a diet deficiency is his resistance lessened.

It has been proven that cage and aviary birds and poultry, nourished with albumin-rich food and vitamins A and B, are better protected against worms and their harmful effects than those birds not nourished in this way. All psittacines need a good supply of grit that must be regularly available to them. One should not simply scatter it on the aviary floor, but provide it in trays, so that there is little danger of the birds picking up worm eggs from the ground while ingesting grit.

The covering of the aviary floor is also important. If the bottom consists of a layer of earth or sand that can be moistened by rain, then it will be an ideal breeding ground for worm eggs.

Therefore a gravel or concrete floor is recommended, as worm eggs soon dry out and die on gravel or concrete.

Never place newly purchased birds in with established aviary residents before making sure that they are worm-free. It is therefore wise, when exchanging or buying birds, to ascertain that they have been duly wormed. In this respect, mutual trust between bird lovers is very important.

Nevertheless, if you want to be absolutely sure about the bird's condition, place the newly purchased bird in an indoor cage. If the bird continues in good condition, after a few days. worm it. To be one hundred percent sure, repeat again ten days later.

It is not absolutely necessary to follow this procedure, indeed not every bird keeper can. The certainty that the birds will be worm-free without a period of isolation is lessened accordingly.

Treating the Worm-Infested Bird

About 15 years ago, a small tube containing a capsule was used to worm birds. This tube, with a rather sharp upper-side, was "forced" into the beak. With much patience (if, in the meantime the bird had not become so frightened that shock was close) one could attempt to push the tube about an inch into the beak. Following that the capsule arrived in the birds' crop through a small hose positioned in the tube. If one was lucky the capsule would enter the crop, if not it could just as easily get into the trachea, which could be fatal. If, in that event, the bird wasn't given a strong shake, head down so that the capsule could be expelled from the trachea, the animal would die.

Fortunately times have changed and there are various reliable and effective products available that are easier and safer to use.

Worms found in parrot-like birds, it has been claimed, will not appear in other avian genera. I personally have my doubts about the above pronouncement. Avoid all risks and use the best wormicide for psittacines, L. Ripercol®, L. Narpenol®, and for the European market, Ovorotol.®

Many modern fanciers know that the syringe or crop-needle is the most popular worming method. To those who are not familiar with this, it will seem difficult to put the crop-needle into the crop of the bird. Some veteran aviculturists still do not dare use this method and will ask an experienced friend or breeder to do it for them.

If you don't like handling the crop-needle, another effective method of worming is dosing with concentrates. I have personally used this method over the last several years successfully, along with "the needle."

If your birds are accustomed to concentrated food, it is easy to mix the vermicide with these treats; the birds will certainly ingest it. Just take the normal portion of concentrate the bird eats within 24 hours and add 1/3 cc Narpenol to it.

166

Tests have proven that an eventual overdose scarcely bothers the bird and should this be so, then only during the first 48 hours.

If you have birds however that refuse concentrates, you will be compelled to use the syringe.

Mixing the vermicide with the food has the advantage of enabling the bird to absorb all the drug. Alternately, when using the crop-needle, some birds vomit the whole lot. In that case it is advisable to keep the bird quietly in the hand so that it won't vomit, waiting till the fluid has mixed with the contents of the crop.

Many fanciers mix the vermicide with their birds' drinking water, but that is the last method I would recommend. This method never gives any certainty. A sick bird barely drinks (unless he has warm lodgings) and as most bird keepers will know, psittacines are seldom found near water containers.

Whatever vermicide you use, repeat the treatment after ten days. By this time the worm eggs at the bottom of the aviary will have ripened and a second phase takes place in the bird's body. After this second treatment the worm cycle has ended, as the worms are not full grown and therefore cannot produce eggs.

This only applies on the condition that the aviary floor is given a good cleaning, refreshing the ground by digging it up deeply to at least 17 inches.

You can also scorch the ground with a blow-torch, a method I personally prefer. Afterward I still dig up the ground to at least 17 inches deep. Other disinfectants won't be sufficiently thorough and I only trust the methods described above.

Observe your birds regularly and when one of them is not well-feathered (outside of the molting period), don't wait until it is too late, but take precautions and measures immediately. There is a good chance that it has a worm infestation and that the bird can be saved.

Other good advice: if you have a sick bird, place it in a warm hospital cage so that it can recover a little and endure the worm treatment better.

A final remark: in case of a severe infection with a bird in great distress, it is advisable to reduce the dosage of vermicide to a quarter of the normal dose. As a large dose kills all the worms at the same time, it may cause constipation of the intestinal canal. Twenty-four hours after this treatment you can give the bird a normal dose, if necessary. After the treatment keep the bird in the cage for several days and give it the best nourishment you can find, for example vitamins and unripe grass and weed seeds.

Worming several times won't harm the bird; this has been proven scientifically, and those fanciers who think that by excessive worming the animals become sterile are wrong. Worming doesn't affect the birds' fertility at all.

Parasites

Parasites can be divided into those which are present *on* birds (ectoparasites) and those present *in* birds (endoparasites). Endoparasites can be found in the intestines, in the blood and in the body tissue. The parasite known as *Coccidia* causes infections in the intestines resulting in slimy, bloody excreta. Your veterinarian can prescribe sulfonamides which will treat though not prevent this condition. The excreta can infect other animals, therefore the most scrupulous hygiene is required.

Mites (ectoparasites) cause "chalk legs." They bore holes, which look like scabs, in the skin of the feet. Apply olive oil or Vaseline to the infected places in order to seal off the oxygen supply to the mites. This treatment will kill off the parasites, but it can take some time before it is effective. Prevention is always better than cure, so keep any infected birds away from the others to avoid the spread of the infection.

Bacteria

The most common form of bacteria causing illnesses in birds is *Escherichia coli.* If anything is wrong with the bird's food, the bacteria, which live in the intestines, multiply rapidly, often resulting in the death of the bird. Sulfonamides are known to be a good cure and can be obtained from your veterinarian.

Tuberculosis

Tuberculosis is caused by bacteria (*Mycobacterium avium*) and infection takes place via the droppings of an infected bird. It can also be caused by bacteria on eggshells or human beings suffering from tuberculosis. To avoid the risk of tuberculosis, the highest level of hygiene is very important. In addition, make sure your birds have plenty of fresh air (without drafts, of course) and lots of sunshine. A bird which suffers from tuberculosis loses weight, does not feed and will show blood in its droppings. If an infection is suspected, separate all of your birds from each other immediately. Don't lose any time in disinfecting your cage or aviary with Cresol, 3% Formalin solvent or Chloramin. Any affected bird will eventually die from the infection because, sadly, there is no known cure for tuberculosis in birds.

Make sure your healthy birds are given ample vitamins and minerals. Keep them separated for a few weeks until it is clear that the infection has been contained. Often tuberculosis appears as swollen limbs. Many an infected bird will die as a result of a tear in the liver.

Dead birds should be burned and not, as is often the case, stuffed because the danger of contamination remains.

Paratyphoid

Paratyphoid is a disease of the intestines, and the symptoms appear in various forms. The most common form is caused by *Salmonella typhimurinum* bacteria, which are also dangerous to all mammals, including

168

humans. The illness subsides quickly with young birds but very slowly with adults. Paratyphoid is often carried by raw egg shells which are fed to birds and is often the result of poor hygiene. However, more often than not, mice and other rodents are the chief culprits for carrying and spreading bacteria. Therefore, you must make sure that rodents are never able to get into or even near birdhouses.

Infected birds have no appetite, shiver with cold and sleep a great deal. The droppings look white-yellow or green as is the case with diarrhea and the vent is very dirty. In acute cases of the disease affected birds can hardly keep their balance and their eyes discharge a slimy liquid. The birds become inactive and lose weight. If their condition improves they should still be isolated. They need to be checked by a qualified veterinarian who will treat them with antibiotics.

Psittacosis and Ornithosis

Also known as parrot fever, this disease can be transmitted to humans (pneumonia). Parrots can suffer from the former which is an illness caused by the virus *Muyagawanella psittaci*. Other species of birds can suffer from Ornithosis which is caused by the virus *ornithosis*. Parrots and parakeets normally carry this illness with them from their life in the wild which is why parrot imports are strictly controlled, with birds kept in quarantine for some time. Affected birds do not want to feed, fluff up their feathers and their excreta is grey-green. If the course of the disease enters its final stage, nervous disorders can be found in those affected. For example, birds can no longer sit on their perches. With antibiotics, it is possible in the early stages to kill the virus and save the birds. But chances of recovery are usually slim with the affected birds dying quickly. Remember that dead birds must be burned. Luckily I have never yet encountered a case of psittacosis in Cockatiels, although, of course, this does not mean that it cannot happen. It will be less likely if the birds are kept away from other species of larger psittacines, especially those of South American origin.

Personal Hygiene

I consider it most important that every bird lover who handles sick birds, sees himself as a potential carrier of infectious disease.

Therefore it is absolutely necessary to wash one's hands thoroughly after touching and handling a sick bird, before going to a second bird.

I have noticed that washing the hands is rarely found in the vocabulary of fanciers, but from now on they should know better!

Rubber gloves must be disinfected and sterilized by boiling after treating a sick bird.

Finally one more piece of advice at the end of this, in some respects, less than cheerful chapter. It is not possible to cover all the health problems and ill-

169

nesses related to Cockatiels in this chapter; the space being too restricted. Every bird lover should have a good book specifically on the subject to serve as his own reference to maintaining health and warding off disease among his own birds. The Bibliography herein includes several excellent works on the subject.

Appendices

MOST Societies publish magazines, bulletins or newsletters for their members. The following national publications are also available:

American Cage-Bird Magazine (monthly)
3449 North Western Avenue
Chicago, IL 60618 (USA)
(features a monthly directory of bird societies)

Avicultural Bulletin (monthly)
Avicultural Society of America, Inc.
734 North Highland Avenue
Hollywood, CA 90038 (USA)

Bird World (bi-monthly)
P.O. Box 70
No. Hollywood, CA 91601 (USA)

Cage and Aviary Birds (weekly)
Surrey House
1, Throwley Way
Sutton, Surrey, SM1 4QQ (England)
(Young birdkeepers under sixteen may want to join the *Junior Bird League*. Full details can be obtained from The J.B.L., c/o *Cage and Aviary Birds*)

The A.F.A. Watchbird—American Federation of Aviculture Inc. (bi-monthly)
P.O. Box 1125
Garden Grove, CA 92642 (USA)

The Magazine of the Parrot Society (monthly)
24, Rowallan Drive
Bedford. (England)

Major Societies

Australia:
Avicultural Society of Australia
P.O. Box 48
Bentleigh East
Victoria

Canada:
Canadian Avicultural Society, Inc.
c/o Mr. E. Jones
32 Dromore Crescent
Willowdale 450
Ontario, M2R 2H5
Canadian Institute of Bird Breeders
c/o Mr. C. Snazel
4422 Chauvin Street
Pierrefonds, Quebec

Great Britain:
The Avicultural Society
c/o Mr. H. J. Horsewell
20 Bourbon Street
London W.1.

New Zealand:
The New Zealand Federation of Cage Bird Societies
c/o Mr. M. D. Neale
31 Harker Street
Christchurch 2

United States of America:
Avicultural Society of America
(See *Avicultural Bulletin*, Pg. 171)
American Federation of Aviculture, Inc.
(See *The A.F.A. Watchbird*, Pg. 171)

American Cockatiel Society
9812 Bois D'Arc Court
Forth Worth, Texas 76126 (USA)

The American Cockatiel Society was formed in 1977 by a small group of dedicated Cockatiel breeders in Fort Worth, Texas. This founding body recognized the need for such a specialty society, dealing with only one species of birds, Cockatiels.

The American Cockatiel Society is truly a national organization. A.C.S. has members and/or officers in all 50 states and several foreign countries. A general meeting is held each year in conjunction with the national show. The show site rotates each year to different sections of the country.

The purpose of the A.C.S.:

1. To encourage an interest and understanding of the Cockatiel as a pet, breeder or exhibition bird;
2. To maintain an official standard of perfection for judging the ideal;
3. To maintain a panel of qualified judges, so that judging will be of uniform quality, governed by the A.C.S. standard;
4. To encourage close banding, selective breeding and record keeping;
5. To increase interest in mutations through study pertaining to the genetics of the Cockatiel;
6. To exchange ideas and inform all members throughout the world by the medium of the *A.C.S. Bulletin*;
7. To support research pertaining to the nutrition and ailments of the Cockatiel;
8. To hold, support and exhibit at the national Cockatiel specialty show each year.

Bibliography

Allen, G.R. and C. Allen. 1978. *Cockatiel Handbook*. TFH Publications, Inc. Neptune, New Jersey.

Barrett, C. 1949. *Parrots of Australasia*. N.H. Sewart, Pty. Ltd.

Barringer, C. 1960. "Albino Cockatiels," *Foreign Birds:* the magazine of the Foreign Bird League, 26: 146-147.

Bates, H.J. and R.L. Busenbark. 1978. *Parrots and Related Birds*. TFH Publications, Inc. Neptune, New Jersey.

Brehm. 1864-1869. *Illustrirte Thierleben*. Volume 3.

Brereton, J. LeGay. 1963. "Evolution Within the Psittaciformes." Proc. XIII Int. Orn. Congr.: 499-517.

idem and K. Immelmann. 1962. "Head Scratching in the Psittaciformes." Ibis 103: 169-175.

Cayley, N.W. 1938. *Australian Parrots*. Angus and Robertson, Sydney.

Courtney, J. 1965. "Down Colouring of Some Australian Parrots." Emu 65: 148; also corrigenda, Emu 65: 317.

idem: 1974. "Comments on the Taxonomic Position of the Cockatiel." Emu 75(2): 97-102.

Curtis, N. 1963. *Cockatiels*. TFH Publications, Inc. Neptune, New Jersey.

de Grahl, W. 1979. *Parrots*. Ward Lock Ltd. London.

de Ross, L. 1972. *Keeping Aviary Birds in Australia*. Lansdowne Press. Melbourne.

Delpy, K-H. 1980. *Der Nymphensittich*. Albrecht Philler Verlag. Minden.

Duke of Bedford. 1969. *Parrots and Parrot-like Birds*. TFH Publications, Inc. Neptune, New Jersey.

Forshaw, J.M. 1969/1981. *Australian Parrots*. Lansdowne Press. Melbourne.

idem: 1979. *Parrots of the World.* Lansdowne Press. Melbourne, 2nd edition.

Frith, H.J. (editor). 1976. *Birds in the Australian High Country.* A.H. Reed, Sydney, revised edition.

idem: 1976. *Reader's Digest Complete Book of Australian Birds.* Reader's Digest Services Pty, Ltd., Sydney.

Freud, A. 1980. *All About the Parrots.* Howell Book House, Inc. New York.

Greene, W.T. 1884. *Parrots in Captivity.* Vol. I. George Bell and Sons, London. All three volumes reprinted by TFH Publications, Inc. Neptune, New Jersey, and updated by Dr. Matthew M. Vriends (1979).

Hall, J. 1976. *Cockatiels . . . Care and Breeding.* Thorndale, Texas.

Harman, I. 1981. *Australian Parrots in Bush and Aviary.* Inkata Press. Melbourne and Sydney.

Hill, R. 1967. *Australian Birds.* Nelson, Australia.

Holyoak, D.T. 1972. "The relation of *Nymphicus* to the *Cacatuinae.*" Emu 72: 77-78.

idem: 1973. "Comments on taxonomy and relationships in the parrot subfamilies *Nestorinae, Lorrinae* and *Platycercinae.*" Emu 73: 157-176.

Immelmann, K. 1968. *Australian Parakeets.* A.O.B. Brussels.

Keast, A.J. 1961. "Bird Speciation on the Australian Continent." Bull. Mus. Comp. Zool. Harvard, 123: 307-495.

Lendon, A.H. 1973. *Australian Parrots in Field and Aviary.* Angus and Robertson. London and Melbourne.

Loeding, W. 1979. *Nymphensittiche.* Franckh'sche Verlagshandlung W. Keller & Co., Stuttgart.

Low, R. 1980. Parrots, *Their Care and Breeding.* Blandford Press. Poole, Dorset. England.

Macdonald, J.D. 1973. *Birds of Australia.* A.H. and A.W. Reed. Sydney.

Mathews, G.M. 1912. "A Reference List to the Birds of Australia." Novitates Zoologicae 18(3): 171-455.

Moon, E.L. 1976. *Experiences with my Cockatiels.* TFH Publications, Inc. Neptune, New Jersey.

Munks, B. 1959. "The Dilute Cockatiel." *Foreign Birds:* the magazine of the Foreign Bird League. 25: 237.

Plath, K. and M. Davis. 1971. *This is the Parrot.* TFH Publications, Inc. Neptune, New Jersey.

Pinter, H. 1979. *Handbuch der Papageienkunde.* Kosmos, Franckh'sche Verlagshandlung, Stuttgart.

Radtke, G.A. 1980. *Die Farbschlage des Nymphensittichs.* Albrecht Philler Verlag. Minden.

Rogers, C.H. 1982. *Cockatiels, Their Care and Breeding.* South Group, Ltd., Leicester and New York.

Sedgwick, E.H. 1936. "Cockatiels and Galahs." Emu 35: 237.

Serventy, D.L. and H.M. Whittell. 1976. *Birds of Western Australia.* 5th edition, University of Western Australia Press, Nedlands, Western Australia.

Slater, P. 1970. *A Field Guide to Australian Birds. Non-passerines.* Rigby Ltd., Sydney.

Smith, G.A. 1978. *Encyclopedia of Cockatiels.* TFH Publications, Inc. Neptune, New Jersey.

idem: 1976. "Notes on Some Species of Parrots in Captivity." Avicultural Magazine, 82: 22-28.

Vriends, T (= Matthew). 1979. *ABC voor de Vogelliefhebber.* Hollandia, Baarn, Netherlands, 2nd edition.

idem: 1979. *Handboek voor de Liefhebbers van Australische Papegaaien en en Parkieten.* Hollandia, Baarn, Netherlands.

idem: 1981. *Papegaaien en Parkieten uit Afrika, Azië and Zuid-Amerika.* Kim/Hollandia, Baarn, Netherlands.

idem: 1979. *Parakeets of the World.* TFH Publications, Inc., Neptune, New Jersey.

idem: 1977. *Prisma Papegaaienboek.* Spectrum, Utrecht.

West, D.G. 1968. "Pied Cockatiels," Parrot Society Magazine, 2: 16-17.

Whitborn, E. and L.N. Robinson. 1962. "Cockatiels Breeding in Southern Victoria." Aust. Bird Watcher 1:225-226.

Whittell, H.M. and D.L. Serventy. 1948. "A Systematic List of the Birds of Western Australia." West. Aust. Mus. Spec. Publ. No. 1: 126 pp.

Books on Bird Diseases

Arnall, L. and I.F. Keymer, 1975. *Bird Diseases.* Baillière Tindall, London, and TFH Publications, Inc., Neptune, New Jersey.

Kronberger, Harry, 1979. *Haltung von Vögeln-Krankheiten der Vögel.* Gustav Fischer Verlag Jena. 4th edition.

Petrak, M.L. et al. 1969. *Diseases of Cage and Aviary Birds.* Baillière Tindall, London, and Lea & Febiger, Philadelphia.

Raethel, H.-S., 1966. *Krankheiten der Vögel.* Francksche Verlagshandlung, Stuttgart.

Vriends, T (= Matthew). 1981. *Ziekten bij volièrevogels.* Zuidgroep, Best/The Hague.